YOUNG MOBSTER

4

SYSTEM DEMOCRATIC

UNIVERSAL

Author   Jaime Vinas

All rights and priviledges over this book had been reserved by his author for which any reproduction, total or parcial over this book, have been forbidden, whitout of the written permission of its author.

4

YOUNG MOBSTER

4

SYSTEM DEMOCRATIC

UNIVERSAL

INDEX

1	08
2	30
3	50
4	87
5	121
6	145

YOUNG MOBSTER 4

DEMOCRATIC SYSTEM, UNIVERSAL

INTRODUCCION

In the previous book, Worm addressed himself to all the world for to get aligned with the rest to close the circle with the Universal Democrstic System, at this moment, all get closed, connecting to the rest of the world in the same marc as the Lord Almighty ordered to be done, until all have the same system administrative with best system over all, where the world be administered under the system more efficient of all, taking the maximum advantage to the resources that in the world could reunite from among all

We should remember that in the previous book Worm also had been in the Africa, reviewing all the work that had been done with the seeds and the animals that he had been sent, that he receive informations of the performance of the labors but he have not been verified the results physically, or by photograps, or videos, only words, then went on a verification trip over those labors, and stood impressed for the results, had done beyond of what he could expect, and much more of all of what is was said to him, those villas in the articicial lakes where not only beautiful and agreebables, were wonderful.

Now is the turn for the rest of the world, they started the anexion for those that less were in need of him, to conclude also with those who are the more in need of help in this moments.

YOUNG MOBSTER 4

DEMOCRATIC UNIVERAL SYSTEM

Chapter 1

Berta and Worm left for their reunion with the president of Europe and were speaking friendly about the system in the isle, how they implanted and were functioning in America, North, Central and South, about the happenings in Africa, and how those were not at charge for any of them, or that they were not taking advantage over them, because the friend Worm took charge for their development over there, that they were already autosuficient, for which any collaboration of them were summarily refused by them, that do not want them not even as visitors, because they would be always to their side, so it be a desagreevable from boths parts.

Worm – That look to me very well really, that always been watching them, because your intellingence is not the most awake, and could need in any moment of your collaboration, when you may need to broad your mind or to consider another proceeding, what I ask you is that to be honest with them, because that is the base that from now ahead will work in order to be able to keep a good friendly relationship with them. They have been abused for you during a long time, and is the reason for them positioned to the defensive with you, have it present, and stay away of diminish them, as you always are used always, so you may keep good relationship with them.

Primer minister of England – And who are you to come to give us orders to us, who do you have believe you are?

Worm – I am not giving you orders, only a friendly advise, because I know that here the important are and always are going to be you, your title of chief is according it looks too much of importance, and it is unchangeable, only I warn you, to leave your title of chief to rest, or it be comletelly not tolerable, Africa is one times more numerous that the united kingdom and your unseparable friend the United States, I know that they do not desire the war, but now can buy the arms for war that they desire because they have a fortune that now have it duly and do not waste it.

President of France – Pardon me mister Worm, since that our friend and neighbor is not seen that is not Africa your poor colony that we need to see it on a new different way and how this have been the reason for the beginning of two world war that we had to tolerate, will not to risk a third, but our noses should look in another destiny, because Africa is past history, and should live it as a free country, no as the continent that we had the chance pinch much before.

President of Belgium — We had a colony over there, they made us a bloody war, a very bloody one, and also we finish loosing it, Mister Worm not leave of to be right, they will fight to dead, who ever dare to intent to take out their freedon, I am completely sure of that, is a theme that we have discuse and analized over there in Belgium, also we have discuse in Holand and Denmark, and all three got to the conclusion of that is a theme of history only, and now the all continent as a single country will be stronger that never in a fight.

Worm — Misters, please, return to our question, that Africa is something in the pass, and that will not get to any different definition, no matter how we look at it, the matter is that our people live with less worries, that the evolving ot the things result every day more with armony, that of what my wife and me came to distract you from that you call your occupations, for you do not ocupaid the less you can, that you handle a small govern, not one that you want to be every time greater, because there are more opportunities, so the members of your party occupied more positions and robe more abundantly to the people. This system come to the point with to eliminate the robes to the people, the people most to be honest, or the system democratic will vomit them.

President of France – Be more kind and make it a little more slowly, how is that the system would vomit to the corrupt, is that this system have included personal audit agains the leaders of the govern?

Worm – No properly, but when someone is dishonest will get noticed from different forms, the money will not be used practically in any place, that from one side, when it be necessary for your country accomplish with your suppliers, are not exact that is not enough? Because the budget are exact, Because the budget are not exact, for which any detour of those will unsquad the balances of the all areas and is how is note of that someone is been unloyal to the system, and the functions are clearly delimitates as for to know inmediatelly where is the dishonest one?

Prime minister English – We do not have great problem with dishonesty, our employees are dign and correct, so we can go ahead.

Minister or Denmark – Same I say, I am positive with your system Mister Worm.

President of Belgium – I can not say the same, but if this system can give a better life to the population of my country, I want it installed already.

Worm – It is alright your conversations, we will see in the practice how it continue behaving, because I know there are much interest what to cut, and there are besides another theme to consider, the president of the isle would be able to give you all the details to follow to be able to start to implement it, I recommend the same that to the Americans, to visit the isle for some time so you may watch with your own eyes in the practice how do the system work over there, the other thing that I would like to is the possibility of Europe be an entire country, because for the end of the world should be a single country any way, this would be to make to our God the labor a little more simple, see it from the point of view, if you wish, but see yourselve in the eyes of Africa, for you also the public administration would be more simple, the public occupation would be more simple, the public administration should not be for simple polititians thieves, but for proben persons, that ocupe their positions for opposition, for their capacity, no for their intrusion in a political party, there will not more political parties, the democratic system do not consider those, will not been more elections in the world, because finally the world is coming to be democratic, where the peoples opinion be the one that prevail.

Giving that way the meeting for finished. Berta and Worm get withdrawal to rest in the hotel where have , fixed a reservation to send that night, inmediatelly call the island where get informed that the next day, in hours of the afternoon start the next meeting in Switzerland, where will meet with a great agroupation of countries, where will be Norwai, Sweeden. Spain, Italy, Greek, the rest of Europe, all are duele motivated, because are convinced of that the system work, that is practical and functional contrary to all the countries of the world, those already went to visit the island, now feel well that they should make that adaptation the way it can be done and as fast as possible.

With that information for advanced go likely to talk in that meeting, that will not ve anymore to motivate them, but to answer any question that they may need or any question that to be of rigor.

Worm – Good afternoon ladies and also gentlemen, produce to me a great pleasure to be among you in this very beautiful afternoon give me a very great satisfaction to be among so much educated and beautiful people as you look like to be are. You all know the reason of my visit to you at this room, I hope by the contrary I will tell you we are here my wife and myself to clarify whatever think that you desired or need to be put in clear to you, someone want to be the first to talk from among you?

Switzerland – We need then to destroy our country to build houses as I saw in the island how you live or is another way in the deep the idea that you are bringing between hands?

Berta – No, do not have to destroy the houses that you have build, only to adapt them so they can be equal more or less the same, so do not go to be some better or worse, do you understand the idea or does it need more details?

Switzerland – No, I think that answered my doubt.

Worm – Does someone like to continue clearing your mind with another doubt you may have?

Norway – Tell me lease, how do you solve the need of money to make international travels, because according I see there is no possibilities to be able to do it

Berta – In my isle, that was something that was made before by the government, and the people did never have need to use planes, I do not know if you have noticed that in the isle there is not international airlines that is due to that the citizenship does not need to make international travels; in the future, you will have in average a trip in plane per week, a roadway for the all country, that would be the only you will need, the tourism is something that belong to the capitalism, and in the democratic system is something that no longer will be used. The all tourist will be internal, your country should consider this and to make structural zones or something similar as for persons have a variety of locations for to enjoy the free time as summer houses or something for the style. Because no longer will need to visit familiars, or to make trips to get to know, because that you can do without need to live home.

Finland – Also us in Finland, are worry for that detail, we travel a lot internationally, and go to see that cut off simply just like that? Will not to be another way to solve this?

Worm – All things have a solution, the remedy of this have two vertients, according I see that, the world will change very soon, and possibly your needs of travel will be affected for those changes, one of those is that you continue like that, and that your government find a solution, and the second is that you just abstent of to do it, which would be probably the best solution.

Finland – This since to be a significative problem for many of those who are in these meeting, because so as we are been affected in this situation, also will be another similitudes, I do not know how this will be solved, will see.

Berta – You were all in the island, went to be received to the airport, and did not see over there and agglomeration of people or anything likes that, better look like a dessert isn't it? The same will be yours, you can not to have it all, something must to be sacrificed, that is on what will happen, will not be necessary into anybody, it will be so much the satisfaction that you would have that little thing will not to be missing for anything.

Norway – For us is not a real need, look like we will not miss it, the only is to me would be to understand what would we can do to expect for the results and then to analize what think is that for us would be important, because says Mr Worm that we will not missed, we do not have any motive to doub from his words, because it is not him is recorring the world? And say that thing is not necessary? What then will happen?

Berta – What will happen is very simple, you will get adapted to the new system; to fly will no longer will not be needed until you get feeders in your body and ails, and when that happen then, you will be flying faster that all you may imagine, that is what will happen, if never they come out, then you will not need either, the planes only are necessary to make international business ot something like that, but when you don't even have a budget to by air tickets for pleasure, does it make necessary to think in something else?

Austria – Misters Berta is not abnormal, or either is mister Worm, they have explained to us that to visit other countries and so, will not be necessary that is something we that we now do, we will have another alternatives. See that way, and If cannot that will be present to anothers as well the same thing, and we will find the solution.

Worm – That may be the final solution, because anyway this is not something that will happen for next day, this will happen many years after implementation definitely. We will not take care of this only, when we are not going to find any solution now.

Hungary – on what I lived in that isle not only I like it, it enchanted me too much, and we are ready to start to build the base to elaborate and to put to work that system in our country ass soon as possible, we started to modify the houses and to prepare the all the burocratic system, the commercial operations and industrials have pass to the state, already those elementals things imprescindibles so the change may take effect.

The continuation of those discussions had its final with some diasagreement, but that each one will resolved to their way in the moment of to aply the new system, but mostly they agree in all the parts, when returned to the isle they were gratly surrised for the way how things were done over there, too simples, could not understand the things that were said before to get over there, it was a pile of surprises what they got.

On the other hand in the president offices were taking care the channel of the next meeting for Worm and Berta, what were including the rest of Europe and some of the countries of the previous soviet union to do with them a pool more adequated and friendly, but equal to how Worm was expecting, while more to the east go, is how more difficult is to dealt with them, because their form to forget the mind and is more distancing, more the latinos and American thinking, he suspect that, and for the way that the world was developing, this was something that he could intuit that would happen and was expecting that was like that. No matter and of course it was not on what he desired.

That meeting is celebrate in Russia, Worm and his inseparable Berta arrived over there, after leaving Switzerland what was a little short reazonable, was in train for a change and to let rest the plane of the Venezuelian president that had been so nice at let them to discontinue using their airplane, and with the bill of expenses also included from the people of Venezuela with wich Worm have an account of gratitude that it would be practically imposible to liquidated but with a great love that he still have for them, maybe it would be enough.

The meeting took place in a hotel that the local president of the communist party had organize from London, making that difficult part to arrive, let the imagination to fly, he never had been in Moscow, not even near of over there, imagine now, to get a saloon where to treat with so many figures, be safely, it would be a job very hard to resolve. Necesarily should be someone with the knowledge of the city, over there, the meeting took place, with the amenity of coffee, tea, that were the drinks used over there, and at the end some vodka, but offer only as a kind of celebration so they did not wanted to the alcohol could bring to call for a disorder because they were not the most quiet of the world, and that had pass many difficult years by the time of the years 20, then with the two world war and then with the resurge of the socialism, a ficticious thing, but to served the base that could order very well the cow of the prusians and men of the zhares that left a protagonist place that took escene of the acts that was of the revolution on the year 1918, when the zars, that were asesinated together with all their families, until the last one, at which exterminated with all the relatives they could ever find, look like there nobody that could claim the greatest fortune in the world by that time.

With all that past, it should be wait that a new change in the political structure basic would not to be easy of to apply, but they got a great surprise, because them, were likely to live in a world as is lived in the isle, in perfect freedom that they always had dream, different than the United States, that proclaim freedom, but they live in a prison more closed than any other place in the world. But Worm and Berta were very far from to think that this could take a happy end and they were radiant of happiness to participate of the motion that finally open the doors of the freedom especially for those of the ex soviet union because that order of ferreous sticky of the communists (Englishman) enclosing more or less open that the all dictators of the poor countries of the capitalists wave.

Worm – Ladies and Gentlemen, be yourself welcome to this meeting, where will treat a theme that for many of you could result in something never saw before, or could be that none of you have had in the pass by your mind to be able to find, so close of yourselves but here I am with my lovely wife, to find an answer to your doubts, until you understand correctly, that this system is the perfect way to live, that the Creator of this world desired that be forever, but that could not be possible, then he sent my father that lived in another galaxie, and for an weird razon came until here, to intent stablish on eart the past plan of God, as a second opportunity for the earth.

Berta – My love if you allow me some words, you all are realize of what my husband realize in the United States, a arrogant country for to accept international help, and so well they did before the sugerence of him, how easy they did to resolve that very difficult that they had, with the global union that aplaqued inmediatelly with that bad of more than 40 billions of dollar in material damages, how to no one of us cost a great effort, but that we act as a true friends. Also could you imagine the dramatic change of Africa, how a small help of his did that tremendous country could awake and could produce all absolutely all on what they need, and still have some more than enough to export, transforming them in an isle country, with a great list of products for export.

President of Rusia – As a country, home for this meeting, correspond me to know to offer a welcome to all my neighbors and ex partners in the ex Soviet Union. Whom together made a great effort to keep alive that union that our partners already were claiming for a freedom and I believe that the reason of the world, because it is already was leaving from our control for which it exploeded and gave the independence practically forced, naturally with not desire, but that we could not keep the catle in our corral, there was, we had to let it go each one to their terrain, but that today we will speak about something more softly and better received, I went to the isle and did like too much what I saw over there, I was not under any kind of surveillance, not even for an hour, and did not feel afraid at any time, imagine, the president of the third greatest country in the world sleeping in the bedroom of a common house, from that lucky and awarded island, is not something inimaginable. And nothing happening beyond of a great welfare, I felt that I was In heaven when was over there talking with the people that do not have anything, that they have the entire life assured, that are not afraid to get robed because what they have all others have it too, and do not need to do that for to have it, they can pick for free new in the stores with not need to pay, they all go the same in that system, is on what wee need all that here are reunited, Mister Worm, it would I have that installed for tomorrow, after this meeting finish?

Worm – Mister president, that is my mission, I did not organized our island, when I was born was on the way it is today, it was my father who did it, I only enjoy ir, and continue his labor, because he is not in this planet anymore, he returned to his own, where he continue with his labor and the sons he procreated over there, my unknown brothers also help him to improve the quality of life as we do here mister president, what I more tell you is that to each word of yous be your desire is what I more import now, because with all that positive attitude that you have in your mind, could start the operations that are easy or few for you may start to for in a few years may have it completelly installed you're the democratic operative system which do not include political elections, where the political campaing is prohibited and only tree candidates can be subscribed to be voted and the elections could take place because the actual president wishes to renounce or be depose from charge for any reason they did, it is a way very stable for the country.

President of Grece – No matter my country never have participated in the soviet union it is very interested in to participate of the new world, from wich mister Worm is in charge, we went some who help in the problem of the United States and also went with Israel and France of who help to rebuilt Africa, and consider that is the job more honorable in the history of the worl, for which mister Worm, protagonist of both, deserve all my honor and my public rekoning, and my public reckoning for both, also for work in the democratic system that your father started, and gave to know to the world, all that you are doing that could say loud that I have a lot of faith in that this will work no matter I could not participated in the meeting done in your isle, but I went to Venezuela and could see on what over there is done, the minister of the exterior relations took me to Colombia to see the advantages they are doing over there, and so well his countries have been installing the system and how happy they all are, as much as the government, that have been reduced to 25% or less, but that nobody have been without work, but by the contrary, all have what to do, the system is super efficient and work wonderfully, they all are happy and want to see Worm again who they consider a truly friend.

Italy – Also we are desiross to instal the system, more on our behalf we are one of the seven great ones, will go a lot better with the system working that in the actual conditions, it is dificul to understand, but is easy to see it working, there are not country in the world that do not have difficulties as have the united in the States. The country second richest in the world, after China, but in the island of there is not beings like that; all have a dign life, and all live in equal conditions.

Worm – what good is to ear you speak like that, with those words and that tone mister President, it produce a lot of joy, because that in the one hundred percent is what my wife and me, that is the essence, and I speak in English, because with the system of automatic traduction is how to talk in tongues, I speak in English and every one o you listen in your own language, those automatic traductors are a wonder, and if Alfonso Nobel would be alive, I am sure that would give to the inventor the maximon awarded, but as he died, we need to wait that a comitee appoint it, then another commission had make the proposal for that, but that is te cruelty of this world that make thinks be on that way.

President of Rusia – Well mister Worm do we have authorization or not to start the execution of the system economical democratic, or still we need something else.

Worm – Mister President, you govern your country and after of Mister Rothschild it is you who order and command in your country, you do not need me to start, understand that you the only need is that the Baron give its consent, I understand, for those little knowledge of economy and political economical and govern structure, is the only that you have still need, I do not play in that you do or not do, I am only for in case you want or need to do it and something do not allow you, to help you on that you may need, Mister Predident, you are in complete freedom of to do what is better for you or for your peole, you may count with our support in all you may need.

President of Rusia – Then, I do not need not even the approval of the mayority in this meeting to be able to start to my people have available a more balanced life and of better mental health, safety in all that influences, this system contain all together.

Berta – Mister President, not ours, nor any of the asistents to this meeting to whom we invite because we are convinced of this is the more sublime life that you may reach, this is the form of life that we have the promise that we will have in the new testament, the contract that the God Almighty have reserved this life style for the life after resurrection, that is what want to implement in this planet, the father of my Worm started with this idea only to lived see how good that is and the good that this may work, that is all, you only need to do it sir. And count with us and our support, that you have for completed, we help you in all that is at our reach.

President of Rusia – If you disculp me then, I need to talk to London, and then start organizing all the paper work to start implementing this wonder, because I am convinced of this is the maximum, this is what was unknown when the world started, it is the most efficient way of to conduct our resources, I am going to do it then.

President of Italy – I say the same that the president of Rusia mister Worm, I will be calling to consult what I may need, or about what may forget, this is very wide and delicated for the commence, so that I know since now that I will need you.

Worm – Remember that we are in the isle for on what you may need, if you want to return and take to somebody with you, or to send some more people, have confidence, if you call before is better, on that way someone will pick you up at the airport, always is better to see than to listen, the eyes hog the limit weight in information, remember that is the way the children adquire its knowledge, they do not listen on what you may say, but make a repetition of what they see on what you do, because they see and imitated. Thanks and good luck.

President of Grece – I really nothing have to do here, I am going to start to work, and same as mine partners, neighbors, because also I am convinced that is what we should do for our grece.

Worm – Mister president of Russia, I almost forget to say that Rotschild approved the United States, so that you also will receive the same approval for sure, that is on what I desire to tell you, in case that you does not know. Because no matter the capitalists are really the communists in front of the world, or better said at their back.

The presidents of the countries in the meating of the soviet union, we should follow the linements of Rusia because at the final over all, we depend from them, so we will do the same they do, with your permission, are going to install the new operative system, with your permission, until later, because friends does not say good bye, but until later.

Representatives of the remaining group – Mister Worm, you have listened all those that have widrawaed, the rest of us, have agreed that only me proclame their voices, and all are in agreement and proclaim their voices and they are in agreement in that give for finished this fructiferous meeting giving a Worm applause to you, and your spouse, and to your president to whom we had among us from our heart, thanks for to invite us to the best of the world, we advance to you the greatest of the success, because not only you, your program will have because is the best we can have, this is on what will be used in heaven after the resurrection, or the life after life, so nothing better we can await, wishes the best, the door of our houses will be always open for you, when you have for good to come to us, for a season, or to stay to live with us, because your house is the all world, is what I have to say.

Worm – Due to there is no to whom to speak in this meting, we give it as concluded, in the understand, what it could be no more successfully, tomorrow we should depart to Iran, where we will have our next meeting, they will not be I hope so comprenhensive as have been you, but while more to the east, more closed mind, and when we arrive to the isles, I hope that it will be a lot more to talk, because are going to be more closed.

Worm and Berta gets retired to spend the night In Rusia, the next day will fly to Iran, where will have their next meeting at about 3 in the afternoon, in its capitol Teheran, this is the correct form of to write the name of it's capital, the names does not should be translated, because bring the confusion of to be another thing, for that date Berta was already thinking when it will be that they will have time to rest, to Worm say that every time that they move from one country is as they were doing something different, as they take vacation, but her does not see it on a different form but that they are doing more of the same for which she say to return to the isle, and on that way take some vacation, that he will continue doing it alone, because that is his work, not hers, then she say her work is to love him and to respect his will, but that she will wish that both take a rest, and Worm reminds her, when has Got taking rest, and he has 5,500 years working with no rest, day and night, and she says. But Got is not made out of meat, he is only spirit.

Berta — My love, it is seven in the morning, the plain for Iran will leave us?

Worm — Mi love, do you remember the president of Venezuela, that one who have a man of the country to do the things? We wil go in the plane that him lend us, for that reason, will not let us, we are sure of to arrive on time, no matter we do not get there early to the airport, no more worry, even more, I am going to call him, no matter here are only 7 in the morning, over there is a lot later over there is goin to be tomorrow, so I will called him.

Worm — Mister President.

Chapter 2

Presidente de Venezuela — That voice look konowed, and the person that use it is very loved by me, would you please to identify yourselve my dear friend?

Worm — With all pleasure my dear friend, with all my heard, that is yours entirely, you have no wrong, this is Worm, who talk to you.

President of Venezuela — What so agreeavable for mine ears, it is the best that have happen to me in months, dear, since your weddings had not ear from you that sutil voice, until now, it is Ernesto who always informed me from your pass, I know now that you pass by Rusia and now, and have you going fenomenally, in your labor as a prophet of God on Earth, had done an stipend labor had Ernesto comented to me, your dear pilot, beside of chauffer, but lets forget about him, I had not solicit him to be my gossip, he does that for him to feel better and to used as an excuse to speak to me of something that not to be himself, is just his justification, but please, count to me, what you can, please, I want to ear from yourself.

Worm – Well mister president, until now all have been same as America, have been very comprehensive, of course that the president of the isle had softened much my labor, he had invited them to the isle and had given all the necessary information. That at to enter the meeting, are all convinced of the convenience, that had make me to past on full day for to finish the meeting, otherwise probably had taking a full week in explanations over there, he first invite them to stay with him a week, at to finish that time, convoke them for me to give them the ultimatum.

President of Venezuela – I am having a lot of placer to listen that information from your own mouth, that thing I now from the voice of the gossip, I wish you the best of the best, please come back to my house when you can, because, do not you take some short vacations, that for sure Berta should appreciate, and we spend some days in Margarita, let see, animate yourselve that you know I am a man of action and happiness, come and have fun that to me also is convenient, I need that, please me one time, rest from that troublesome meetings, what do you wait from, come and lets pass some days of happiness all together, the minister will also come, I have him in front of me and do you know he is very happy, he is distributing the wine of don Manuel, the wine that is produced In Africa at the north, and them told him that when you return here will celebrate with you and give you a couple of cases and put that in their account of them, so also he father's friend of the minister also told me that first have a dinner in his new house, and then go to Margarita.

Worm – Mister president, the tentation is great, you are convincing me, and over here there is some one that was talking about that, a few minutes ago, I think we will go she is feeling with emotions mister president, that is taking a sensational form, she wants to salute you by the way.

Berta – What a great pleasure is to salute you mister president, you are converting in our good father at more to be our good father on our wedding, is beside my savior, because the truth I am exhausted of so much thinks, the men does not understand that the women are not that strong to support all that work that support a man, that we need to rest, from time to time, but thanks a million for to convince to my worm, my dear father, because as God took away mine, look like game you for to substitute him.

President of Venezuela – Two tears are running down from mine chicks from mine eyes Mirs Berta, your words have me emotional so much, a daughter that is on what I have be desiring since a long time ago, you do not know how much pleasure I have to hear you talking like that, of course that are you our very dear daughter, because since mine have grown up, I have no love from anywhere, as if have lost them, and thanks for to come to me to share with mine sons this season that will be unforgiven for me I do not know what I will do for this difficult meeting that anticipated that will be difficult, I will want that you will come to over here, that do not even have it. But I wish you that you go even better of that you hope, and expect, and to be with us to spend together those agreevables moments.

Worm – We will do what to be at our grasp that God may depare to us some invitees as the Russian that in one hour already desired to go to work in the proyect. Until soon, that I am feeling that those vacations will filled me up, are fulfilling my energy for the next.

Berta – Good morning mister president, we are calling to solicit a personal favor, is that the president of Venezuela has invited us to spend some time of vacations in the isle of Margatita and we want you to postpone the next meeting in which you are actually working to leave us the next week off, so we may take some vacations, and on top of that we desire that you also come, because we have a fenomenal idea, that will come to the final plan we had done, and that we wil enjoy even more.

President of the isle – The president of Venezuela is a great friend of mine, we spoke over the phone very often, so that pass to pick me up when going to over there, because for sure that we will past a good season over there, not all in life is work, the diversion is one of the parts more important of to be alive.

Berta – Hello, for sure that we will pick you up when going, but please, get you by surprise over there, with your wife, do us that favor, is that we want to pay to the minister of exterior relations from Venezuela, the present of honey moon, and you are enchanted for that.

Worm – Mi love, I think that Is being the moment to depart, I just spoke to Ernesto and he was informed at respect, he has 15 minutes that he is ready and waiting for us in the airport to depart.

Berta – Well, everything is already packet, the major part not even was taking out of the luggage, only spend a single day when we prognosticated that could last four of five days. When you command my owner, because you know that I am your love, and this have an owner.

Worm – Good morning Ernesto dear friend, how do you feel today? I do not see you since Switzerland, I have fortgotten of your smiling face, that soft smile that look in your face, that make you as to be a man sympatique and of agreeable conversations.

Ernesto – karamba, I miss you a lot, but the Russian did not allow me that were too much, because they finish very soon, what happen, I saw them to leave that meeting one by one, they were surprised, what did not like the idea, or there was another reason, because almost all were talking about something over their cellular radio phone, and were seen imparcial, that nothing were affecting them, were not furious, nor even were happy, tell me please, what was that happen over there, please.

Worm – I spoke to the president of Venezuela, who told me that you have been passing information of all that we do over here, and each word that you listen goes retransmitted to him inmediatelly, that must to stop Ernesto, he is a friend, but this is a job that I do, and should not be public information, the decisions of every country is something that only concern to them, and may consider that is me who is supling information, and is for that, this informations should not to be transmited to any one out of those nations, if you want to call your boss, tell him informations about me or Berta, but not with informations of the other countries, stop that he may be entered from the newspapers, when those countries give their own declarations that they want that the world to know, not with mine, please, if you do again, I will send you to Venezuela, because I can pay my own plane, I have all the money that my Lord God have give me, and will do if you do not depose your attitude.

Ernesto – I apologize mister Worm, have the security of that I did not understood what I was doing, did not considered that could bring consequences to you, please forgiveme, it is not going to happen again, I promise to you.

Berta – If those countries may acuse Worm of to be an spy and to loose the confidence that until now we have wom, we go back to the isle, and from there to Venezuela directly, not for any personal think, Ernesto, that could be even dangerous, are persons that have been in war the all life, the history marked like that and who knows the attitude that they could take if that information goes for over there, they could consider that way you are passing information about the meetings, all of us, could be spies, as we have their doors open, could get straregic informations yours, and to pass to their enemies, and put them in great danger, or small danger, but that is something that they do not allow to happen, please, please us, that could be dangerous.

Pilot – I told to your husband to forgive me that will never happen again, I promise you, because the man should not swear.

Worm – The man yes, may swear Ernesto that should not to do is to do it in false, do not swear me for something that anyway you will continue doing, and I tell you, if I discover you do that again, that will be your last day around me, I will put another pilot in this plane for to take you to Venezuela, that is all, we can we now depart please, so we do not get be late.

Ernesto – Sure friend Worm, and please forgiveme, that will not happen again, you have my word as warrantee on that.

Prime minister of exterior relations. Welcome mister Worm and your distinguish wife, hope you feel in our country same or better than in the one who is whitness of your bird, because as your is this country as the one of your bird, be yours very welcome, to this land over the protection of Allah.

Worm – Karamba mister minister, you talk as a truth politician with a great category, I am not used to be treated with welcome words, that is done to a distinguish person, and a special being, for me and my wife, Tanks for your welcome and your eloquent receivement, gave me too much placer to be here in this great country, cradle of very important kings in the pass, and of very important figures of the present time.

Minister of Iran – I have a special car for you, which will left to you for you to be used while you stay over here, while you will stay on this land, also count with an Iranian chaufer who know perfectly the country, for to transport you, in your dayly visits to work, and also in your visits of diversion as a tourist because I would like you to know our country, at least part of it, I hope you have separate time for you in this visit, if you have not do that, we would like to have you again soon, for you to please us in our desire to get you to know our country, we have many beautiful things and that make us proud for them, no matter they do not look in front of your eyes so beauty, please.

President of Iran – Welcome to Iran be you two, mister Worm and your wife miss Berta, we are highly grateful for you to dignify us, the couple most important in the world in these moments, that have dign of to visit our country so humble as ours, to propose to improve, in the most important for our government as for the population, hope that our minister have treat you with al the courtesy that you deserve people that deserve the good, to the humanities all, we are in antecedents.

Worm – Mister president, we humblly appreciate your elocuent words, which look addressed to another person, and not to us, that are really nobody that we are going by the world accomplishing a divine mission, not to mention our words, but the word of God, because is what he had decided for the world, to give another chance, another opportunity of to regenerate, to live better that you may live, with a great joy of the all good that he had created for us all, to those that he had considered always as his sons.

President of Pakistan — Mister Worm, we think good that you be with us in the company of you love the most, but in order to address to us, we want to warn you that do not even intent to treat us to make us discuss our ideology or ours, if you are obedient to God that actually is the same as ours, treat on that way and make out of this meeting to be friendly and finish with a happy end and with harmony, because want that his sons all as are you and are us, to live in friendly and harmony, that we treat all as truly friends, that is the way in which have come, and is the form in which we want still remain, and to continue to stay, and to continue and go the same way, please, have no doubt, we will not disrespect you at any moment, peace for you and for us.

President of Arab — I think the same way as the president of Pakistan, but already those words have been pronounced and the answer have been gaved, beautiful words yours mister Worm that for the others are relaxers for us, peace is a word of which we are unknown, but think that we think that you are coming to treat us, you want us to get to know and we should tell you about it is that it is welcome be, because peace is something new and be unknown for us, but that we always look fot the desire of to know it.

Berta – Thank you very much for your honesty and for your support, we now feel better and more relaxed.

President of the emirat Arab united - Mister Worm, the only thing we want to ask you is that we disered that you please us on that is that you do not let your wife speak, our woman do not tell us what to do, we are men who put the rules and the things in order in our houses and business, so she does not feel bad, we would like to sugest that let her to reunite with ours in the saloon next to us, and pick her up when the working day finish, please, do not get yourself offended, and please respet our costums, please us on this, will make us to feel more comfortable.

Berta — This is absurd, but you ask me that, will go, how can they be so chumsy, is that they do not know that all were born from a woman and that with a lot of pain they should respect that feeling.

President of Yemen — Please Miss Berta, we are all conscients of that is like that, but even us think that the leader should be only one, and that is the man, because Allah made man, then the woman, for to help the man in the things to do in the house, she was not make to direct the man, that is why we ask to our women to let our place for us, and that their occupied theirs, please we ask, await for us in the next room, and let treat this matter with your husband, we supplicated that, as our dear guest that you are, remember that where you go you do what you see, and what you see and will see is that the women do not command in the arab world.

Worm – Very well, understand perfectly, the participation that you give to the being that gave life to you, that is your custom, which will last until the system to be implanted, since there, you will start to give a mayor freedom to the women, we respecting your actual customs, but understand that the rest of the world will not tolerate much this situation, the woman that one who gave you the life, those who cook for you to eat, those that give you pleasure in her companies, very desired by yourselves, those lovely, that to stay awake if you give reason, that do not eat if you make her to suffer, that who always have an smile of hope and happiness for you, that to need a mayor participation in your lifes, and do not tell me that you know it, because you know it for even, from all the possible ways you know it they have communicated that, too much they know that you do not desire to change, because are you who have the dominion, what about if it be upside down, if were theirs who have the control, do not you like that to gibe more freedom? Is that you never have occupied their places to consider in that, we do not put you any imposition, but is not from human to do that? What we are going to implore is to reconsider and give them more participation, that your treat to them to be more lovely, that they at least have the freedom to choose to who they desire to love? Lets see then, please my love, go and await for me in the next room with the other women, please, we need to pacify them and to please them, only for that, go my life, and wait for me this well solve very well.

Berta – It is allright I will wait over there, in silence because I do not speak their language and they have no traductor, they speak the same language, yes my life, I will do for you, and will be in my mind and in my heart.

Worm – Well sirs, my wife is not in the meeting, I took her out to please you, but I have a work to do here and need to have you in peace, not that you are correct, but that I need you in peace, and I am never going to tell you what to do or to impose you my conditions, afortunatelly that form of treat the womens of yours, I do not share it, and how will be so distint, either have to see them, any way, that territoty is very desertic, for your bad behavior, God damaged it, so do not invite me to come for a ride around here either, so peace to you on my side, for sure that I will not introduce myself in your way for that side, will not come back to take that theme; you will do what find better for you, will not stay for to be right.

President of Afganistan – Mister Worm, thanks for to leave the theme of the women, well, get back now to the theme of the meating. We some did not go to the isle to see physically, but we have talk with persons over there, your president on the other hand, was busy and could'nt speak with him, so we need an explanation about how is that it work and then we can make an evaluation and to take decitions about.

Worm – Very well, will start from there, I was treating with you have gone and was treating you as you all had gone over the island, and known how the system work, as you do not have the information you will have it from my mouth, is about over all to produce work all for all, and to be independent from another nations as much as we can, with that porpouse it is needed to create an environment of pulcritud and certain limitations, for example, why to have 50 factories of mayonnaise? If at the end is all the same, that may be seen as a barbarity, with one or two kind producing maybe different taste of maybe different in some that like to different formulas some different to please different taste is enough, why to import 200 kind of automoviles, if with two or three models is more than enough? And to manufacture instead of to import, what I always remember as an example is the form as Mexico implement the manufacture of the most of the things that they produce today, they made an invitation to the different manufacturers of automoviles, refrigerators, televisors, electrodomestics in general, all that they did not produce over there, and offer then exonerations of all kind, gave the terrains, build the needed buildings, and deliver all for free with no titles, an offer complete wide, for 20 years, after of such time they should go and Mexico keep all they gave to them, an offer really attractive and after the period, Mexico kept all, and they went home with empty hands, one of the condition is that they must to use Mexican laborers to perform the work, so when they left all the laborers stayed, and derailed trained, and all of the buildings, land, equipments machinaries, and now they have in house all the manufacturing for all they use before to import, and now are home made, it cost to them 20 years of time to wait, but at that end, they did it, got free of the benefits of the manufacturers that further ahead were Mexicans already, and things like that we can implement for ourselves.

President of Pakistan – I either could have the information from the island, or how is that you do not handle money, how then buy all they need?

Worm – Have not tell that is a very efficient system? They all work for an institution, the government is the owner in the practice, not in the legal, the government take all the productive sector and produce what the country expend, is not an extense government, but it is efficient, nevertheless do not pay regular salaries to its workers, do not collect taxes either, a very low cash salary is paid to the workers, so they still can purchase the thinks that are not for free, as licour, and any think that are imports from another place, same will happen with you, that some things you manufacture and the other manufacture something else, and ad the end you make a kind of change, you give what I need, and I give you what you need, and pay nothing at the end, in such case it come to be as a local manufacturing, because is an exchange for something produced locally, and is why the salary is very low, the people go to the different stores and they get what they need for free. That is in exchange for they labor wicht money they even receive their labor is also an exchange for the things they need, the states that work by that system are superavitaries, produce more that its value in your salaries and it constitute the reserve, that in the long term, is going to finish in the pocket of the citizens, for that we are all happy.

President of Oman – And how then function your enterprise, which we understand that have made you a very rich man?

Worm – That is something a little different, the people of my country do not pay for that, my personal gains are for the exports that we realize, the govern pay me what the people expend, because in this model I work as a vendor, the employee used for that also get in cash, not too much, because the greatest part go to the government because is a revenue from a product that go to export, so the gain goes to the state in cash or in imports from the same country that we do as an exchange, for that reason, my business are not personal, I only manage that, but it works as if I be the govern myself. It work as the government directly, I must to provide information of the all operations to the state. My employees are like anybody else as well.

President of yemen — No matter what you say, the history of the queen of Saba that visit the king Solomon of Israel was originally from my country, when she return to her country with his son David, move to Etiopia and it was over there that the buildings were erected the things that Solomon ordered to build, she later have more childrens, males and females, then changing the theme, mister Worm, for the quantities that your serape is selling, you possible have overpass the richness of the Rockefeller, because that represent many millions, to go over the rich farmaceuticals of the world has not be nothing easy, also you may have an explanation for that for sure.

Worm — Sure I have it, that was something that came from my heart, and I suspect that God himself wanted to give to the world some kind of release, elixir that consist in fruit juice that I use from the fruit harvest in our country, and concentrated juice imported from Brasil, you know that I import big quantities of concentrated juice from Brasil, you know now that I import big quantities of coffee from Brasil, and a little quantity from Colombia, also, we plant cocaine in our fields, and how it is for medicine, it convert in legal cocaine we produce in the country sugar, and those are all the ingredients of the serape, that only is bless from God, and cure all kind of sickness that any person may have, and over it I compete with the farmaceuticals in price, no sir., the farmaceuticals charge for how much a life value, we sale the serape at how much cost a refreshment drink when you buy a medicine in 20 dollars, you may buy a refreshments for 0.10 dollars plus is also some kind of vaccine, I am going to count to you something that happen to an admiral of the united States, he was drinking the serape in a bar, the only that there are in my country, over there was also my brother Roberto, who was drinking a beer before go to dinner, and was where the admiral told him, you came here to moke over us? You are drinking on what your government has ordered you to destroy, in front of all of us, and he answered not, that on any way, he was drinking that because it was a beautiful when his wife was sick, and could not find the cure until a friendly hand offered me a bottle of that elixir that was enough for her to restablished for complete, that he wanted was to find the mobster that he knew that there was in the island, so he have the kindles of make him the favor of take his life, then as the mobster was me, I told him that if he took su much of the serape that my brother said he did, he is immune to dead, and nothing was that I could be done to please him in that porpuse, until the effect finish and that will last months.

President of Iran – Very well mister Worm, what happen then with that admriral, please tell us more about that interesting story, please.

Worm – I took him for a ride, and asked where had him left the float that broad him to the isle, and he told me a place, but the float was not there, and then I explained to him that what happened is that his heard belong to the isle because he was enamoured to dead of it, and that his wife and his two children were in the way to the airport to come to the isle in a plain that myself sent to pick them up to come to make company to him, from before to know you, they should reunite with you at first hours in the morning and live in a house that also will be build for you briefly, we have living over there some thousand persons from the United States, that when they knew the freedom of the living over there they decided to stay, a country where there is not police, or army, or marines, or air force.

President of India – Congratulate you mister Worm, are you a person who express himself very clear, and have an idea that would be the salvation for many, but for India I am not sure that it work very well, because we have too many inhabitants and are a very poor country. What is that we could do?

Chapter 3

Worm – I understand that you were in the island and saw our standard of life, how all live over there, as if were rich, in a capitalist system that is due to we are not too many people, as you are, I think that the first step would be to consider a less level of life as us, that will make that the most poor, have it at the grasp of their hand, another think that you could consider is to forget of the form in that the world have order their economical system and order yours at your way, because the economy is relative and depend of the angle of sight. We will continue rating your case mister president, and we help you in whatever you may need, please have faith, remember that we are on your side, and will help you in all that you may need, have faith, and think further ahead, with a positive mind.

President of India – Then mister Worm, you think that we could also enter in that program? Could we have that hope?

Worm – Do not have you the minor doubt of you can, and not only that you can, you will do, because we are here for that all the countries of the world can live under the plan of God, is that he have desired always, since the creation, until our days, and to honor him we will do it. Mister President have faith, because that is the only thing we need for now, only that.

President of Iran – For what I have ear in relation to the program in India, what they may need would be only not to be so ambitious to start to build the living houses a little smaller, than those you have in the island and to put less expensive equipments inside of the houses, maybe not to put central air conditioning, that the furnitures be more simples, thing like that certain mister Worm?

Worm – Very truth mister president, that and only that would be the solution for them, and also would be for China, Africa, we are waiting for those that first define their internal economy to be more precise into measure the kind of structure that they are going to be able to afford, before to get into it. and other countries that we found out of focus in their habitational structure, because we all qualify, we will see that is like that, according I see, what is needed is that we need to start to build in every country, we are all agreed and what take now is to be all agreed on what we need and to put some simples hands to the work.

They decided to finish the meeting and every country should analize their conditions to see how much they can afford to quantify how much they can build and what should be the life standard they standarized should build for the good life they can give to the population. The North American style for certain did not started as it is now, it was growing little by little with the time, and they still have not rich the life style of the island, and it is the way every country should consider to start. Worm was to the encounter with his love Berta, ask her how she spent the time and she ask to him that sat there watching the others and how to they behave because she did not understand how they do, or what do they said, only said something and laugh loud that give to understand that they are happy with what we think that is incorrect, but that was the way that the Almigthy God structure the world, that was the women under the men power, they only obey his rules and all goes well, said Ismael that the meeting could prolongued for much more time, but that he spoke and work for it to finish ass soon as possible.

Berta – I need to thanks for that great detail because is very boring to be along a group of women educated, without to participate with them, in any thing, because until the games that they did were unknown to her.

Worm – My love, I have a great notice, after that boring is awaiting for you a great diversion, spoke the president of Venezuela for to confirm the invitation for Margarita again, the minister of Colombia, the president of the isle, the president of Colombia, the minister of Venezuela, you can imagine the great party that will be armed over there.

Berta – My life, how could you give me better news, we will reunite with all those friendly persons to whom we love as to own family, only we need Roberto, your mother and aunt, ount you like give that pleasure to them?

Worm – Why no, I will call Roberto right now, to see if they get up and is possible that we take them also. Roberto, I am calling you to make a question, do you have the warehouse and the plantations under control over there?

Roberto – Yes little brother, yes no have worries for that, all is going well. . .

Worm – I am not worry, what I want is to ask you, and depend of that answer, do you have someone that you can put in your place, so you can take a week of vacation very good with us?

Roberto – Yes, I think we can live in charge to Juan, he act hear as my assistant and several times I have commissioned him to go in my place and supervise the plantation and when I get out he stay In charge until my return, and never need to reproach for anything, because always put care in the details.

Worm – Then, free yourself of all, because I am goint to the island tomorrow, and we are going in one or two days for Venezuela, please let know to mama and aunt, so they can come along, is going to be a season that we remember surely for life.

Roberto – How good my brother, I have a girl friend already, here things are improving every time, is a girl from a very good family, the most beautifull girl in the island, not just for her face, or body but for her good modals and refined education, when you come will speak to her, because you already know her only that you do not know your as family yet, but things are going very well among us, to my mother that do not like is that she is going to be alone, so I have think that she come to work in the warehouse, that if she does not help at least will make an space here, and life will result more easy filling herself in certain company from the actual workers in the warehouse.

Worm – How many good news you are giving me, I should involved you in the business a long time ago, because you have done a truly success in your labor, I am very proud of you, now will get involve in more international relations, beside if you can take your girl friend, will pass better moments, try to see.

Roberto – That is something in what I need you to help me out, her fathers are not in accordance on that, and doubt very much that they will concent could be otorgued by myself over all for that she come pregnand from those vacations and for those razon, I would like to asked you if that is not be too much, to accompany me to make that petition, because I am convinced of that to you if going to more difficult to denied, they will concede her to you for me, do me that little favor please, yes?

Worm – You know that I will do, do not you to get shy, that if they do not lend her to us, we married you and we take you as a honey moon trip, now you see?

Roberto – Is for that reason I love you dear brother, you always find the way to get whatever it be happier.

Worm – you know that I love you, and also that you are under my protection, you are my only brother I have, your girlfriend is going to be my first sister girl, so mine is yours too, you will know how wonderful is to have a wife, when she love you besides.

Berta – It look like we do not have any hurry to go, I see you so calmed, that I do not know when do we will go for our country.

Worm – So well, not, I do not have a plan with the details, nothing specific are there for to depart; we are officially on vacations, so we should not be in a lot of hurry.

President of Iran – Mister Worm, how good that I found you, that you have not depart yet, I wanted two things one is that I wanted to thank you for to invite us to form part of this wonder of system that is forming to globalize the world, and the other is do we have to rend account to you or to the president of the island about the steps we should go by or not?

Worm – You are independent, you may have the freedom to do on what you find better, whitout that we even to know, only need from us in order to help you in case something comes up that you do not know how to fix, and we with your help will find the solution so you can make it, only in order to help you mister president, we do not need and does not want to get involved in the questions that is only to your concern and only to you, this has not been the idea of our intent, you are free from us, and we are not thoe that are globalizing the world, only that we want that the all world can enjoy on that way so healthy of life that we have here, that is something that when you have the confidence of communicate with us each time you need or desired, to talk or for inquitants or simple for to talk, we are over all your friends, as if we were your relatives.

President of Iran - You are a truly friend mister Worm, thank you very much for to give me that peace to my spirit, my assistant was wrong if you are an spy yanqui or not, and is the principal reason of this phone call, but you have clear that completely.

Worm – Mister President, have you forget that we had a war against the Richs of the world because they wanted to eliminate God's medicine on earth to continue to robe and poisoning to the people with their poisoning things. My country and the United

States are not the best friends, they intent and got allied with anothers worse than them in order to destroy us, how think you that I can get allied with them to make damaget to another? I personally was , the reason of that conflict because it was my plantations and factory that they considered the enemy, do not you think that something could be a reality, not even in dreams, peace to you.

President of Iran – Once again I ask you to pardon me, it does not come to happen again, I have you as my best friend since now, as my distant relative but I love you every day more, and last time pardon my bad thinking, and those from my assistant

Worm – No, mister president, I owe thanks to you for your honesty, and for to put in clear things as a friend should, do not you fell afraid for to act correctly, because to the truth always will come to the light as the morning start, always bright in the firmament, which will disappear before the end, After the thowsand years with the kingdom of heaven.

Berta – don't should we to leave from this hotel if we are on vacations? Because anyone may come with something if he has any doubt will be calling you, when then will be our vacation starting? Or have you forget how was I treated those commanders that think themselves commanders potentated.

Ernesto – I am in the lobby mister Worm, in case you may need me, you know.

Worm – oh, very well Ernesto, thanks for you to call me, and remind me, Berta is here ready since a long time and making me a great hurry to depart, is the plane fixed and ready to depart?

Ernesto – Those missing are you alone, nothing else the plain is ready, only empty because you are who fille it up, when you want get the trip ready, only get into the plain, and we will go, good, first to the car and then to the plain.

President of India – Mister Worm, I wanted to say good bye to you, and would like to accompany you to the airport if you give me that pleasure, would appreciate very much.

Worm – Sure mister president is going to be and intinite pleasure to be in your company for some more moments, of course yes, come to our car where we will feel more likely, at least us, because are used to it already this is not ours really, what happen is that we had found many friends in this way, this car, and the plain are property of the president of Venezuela, who we are going to reunite in a few days to spend some vacations together with the minister of exterior relations, the president of Colombia, the Minister of the exterior of Colombia, the president of the isle, my brother, my mother, and my aunt, and we are going to have a very good time together, we will make a stop in the island first to pick them up, will salute to the friends, and in a couple of days after to urine some beers that we drink over there, we will go to those vacations.

President of India – That is a faboulous plan, with the new system the president will take some vacations, I presume, because the world is very boring if we only work mister Worm, I was thinking that you only worked, that never rested, but now I realized of that your life is more vacation than to work.

Worm – Is what the aparience shows but that are not practically vacations, but pleasant meetings of the same work, because on what do you think that is going the president of Venezuela and the Colombian one, to vacation or not, they are going to question me something about the system that they need in order to put it to work, to whom do you think they will be waiting to consult? To me, really will enjoy being over there, and in that company that I want, but is going to be more work than vacations, I can assure you. The president have make arrangements for the next meeting and is going to be now when the work, because until now we have treat people who think as us, but as more to the east we go more different to us they are the beings that we will find, for which more difficult will be our work to get communicated.

President of the India — Mister Worm, it is been a great pleasure get your accuaintance, now I say good bye, now I wish you a very good trip back home, so your vacations start very soon, enjoy very much, and please always have present that you let a friend in what since now is your own country beside your other one.

Worm — Thank you very much mister president, I am not going myself, no, my Berta are taking your brothers, because you are like my family since now, I let you full of our affections since today and forever, because you came to us with your affections, and of that I live you full, because more than those you brought you are taking with you, I hope, because we do not take you away, but we put more instead, until always.

Worn, Berta and Ernesto depart in the route to their loved island, giving for finish this broad for the world, living pending for a future date the continuation of this important labor every time moved more to the east, where now will correspond to the countries that they are living in the middle, and north, the suffered Nepal, the big China, the Vietnams, the Koreas, those countries are the future meeting of Worm and his lovelly Berta while the moment comes, they are going to return to their loved isle, to have a brief rest and to visit to your very dearest new family of Venezuela and Colombia.

Berta – Mister president, we are in the air, and going over there in this moments sir, we pretend to honor an invitation for Margarita island after to rest for a couple of days over there, and would like very much, that you and your wife, Worm we did not have the opportunity to share duly, will accompany us, it will be with the presidents of Venezuela and Colombia, the minister of the exterior of both countries, and don Manuel, the owner of the vineyard, that produce those wines so delicious that we like so much, please accompany us, will you?

President of the isle – hello my dear Berta, what agreeable moment to listen your voice, thanks for to take me into consideration for those plans of you, I like very much de idea, you are coming and and will spend some days here. That will make more easy for me, because I am tide here but will finish soon, it can precisely some two days, and after that I will be liverated, so give opportunity to my successor so he goes taking experience in the job and not to be so rude his commence, here we talk more and get more details but would like to spend some days free, thanks for to invite me.

Worm – Mister President, always that my father is so far, you are like that for me, because you have the experience that I do not have, and I need you very much, we love you like that, as you be our natural father please, you do never give us alone, please, we count on you.

Ernesto – Please, wear the seat belts, because I can see the airport and will be landing in a couple of minutes, please every one have a seat with the seat belt assured, we are arriving to the critical moment of the trip, assure yourselves please.

President of the isle – Hello my dear sons, the Lord has prepared a reward for us, to me and to my wife with to give us two sons, that way I felt as happy of that Worm and Berta called me father and be needing me, that have filled me the enthusiasm for to come to receive you at the airport, because you have make me so much needed that did not want to wait until to you show up, I have bring with me to Roberto, Miss maria, and Miss Ruperta, so nobody you will miss, that may interrupt those family minutes, that I miss so much longsickness have given to me, it is very important to feel among a family, and since I am a little oldy already, want to start to share a little near of you, my dear sons, your mother and aunt are like to be mine sisters, Roberto has already behave as to be my own son, I have bring to the future president that will take posesion very soon, in a matter of a few days and to substitute me in this trip of family vacations that we will take, I did like you to know him, because he has manifest to me that you have treat much and well, and as you are so closed to the government, it is very important to know deeply, and that he knows the kind of person that you are, Worm and Berta, so you can to get communicated always on the same form.

Worm – We here talking about the president of Venezuela, and here is coming a plane that look too much to the one we where going by the middle east, if that is not him it should be someone in his plane, because even the matricula is the same, so there is not the minor doubt, that is his plane about the content can not talk yet, but it is very important to arrive to be able to affirm something securely, soon we will know for sure, soon we will know in a minute will land.

President of the isle – Worm my son, you have been to see in many details and that plane on last time, at so that not to be very wrong, presume that you have all the reason for to have all that information to your dermy.

Worm – I see that the Lord have remembered us, have bring to a putative father, have bring likely the rest of our natural family and some friends, now only need to the president of Venezuela to show up with his surprise already used to, because is like have been acting, and we think is like his modus operandi.

President of the isle – Look my son maybe you brought with the thinking because there is his plane, ant to my poor way to judge, it look very much to the one that brought you to over here, it will be that from the same family, have been purchase together?

Ernesto – He purchase the company of Maracaibo, that is possible to be him, I will call him by radio to confirm, I have to move our plane because is park it in the mid of the roadway.

President of Venezuela – Worm! I know that we will see In a few days to pass it together, but did not want to hold on more, the desire to see you, beside I need to talk some points with your president and my wife desired too much to see the lake that you have in the center of the isle for romantic persons that you have over here in the isle, so that I brought for all that, we decided that the best we could do is this, and here we are.

Roberto – I am Roberto, Worm's brother, and will take you to the lake when you liked, here I have my truck and is to your disposition.

Worm – Go mister president, you here do not depend only from me, you have a all family, my mother, and my aunt will not going to like you to say they are sisters, but to Roberto does not import no matter that you are his father, no matter putative, because you have the age to do it, and second, you love us, but no matter here is where you have your family and your friends, what I do not know is what do you do in Venezuela, far away from who love you.

Spouse of the president of Venezuela – Let's see my love when is going to you are going to dedicated me some time, because the fact of that God had reward us our own sons, I think, that is not for you to punish me, no pleasing to whom is sleep less for you have your desires especially my body every night, that never have fail, when will you take me to know that romantic lake for lovers that they have here, and I have so much diseres to know, so we build one in Venezuela?

President of the isle - Over there is Roberto that has offered to take you over there, when the ladys feel ready we can talk about that but to the woman we must to please because they are our principal reason of life, from them we are born, for them we live, with them we share our happiest moments, so, when will you please her? Will you wait until she explodes, and that will not like you?

President of Venezuela – Then, Roberto, shall we live? Because all are going to be against me, if we stay here, this may be a boicot, besides that also, I want to go over there to pass some moments over there, with Warm's wedding I miss her a lot when we went to that place, that for a little more and send the pilot to bring her to over here, it falt just a little to do it.

Roberto – You should to have it done that would be something extremely romantic for her, you can not imagine how much she could thanks to you, for sure that she would be pay for the fare from her own pocket the cost of the trip.

Venezuelian's president spouse — Yes, especially that I do not have pockets, so how could put money over there? Would not pay anything, but could give him like two hundred thousand kisses, beside that if that place is so agreeable as said, I will give anyway, because it was not counted over there, it was him who told me that when he saw me naked in our bedroom he waited that we were as Adan and Eve before to tell me that, today he will not see me under those conditions, because over there it will not happen.

Miss Maria — My dear little Worm, allow me to kiss you and to caress you, hope with that, Berta get a little jealous and also want to do it.

Berta — I what do not know is what is Worm waiting to take me to the lake of the love ones, because I told him when we were in Cape Town that he was not in love with me, because did not want to stay romantic with me, only to talk of business and nothing else, that put me furioss, and still I do not know what does he wait here, I know that the president we owe some time, but we will be a all week together in Margarita, the lake will stay here, and in Margarita there is no lake.

President of the isle – My love, in sight of here this group will go to the lake, I think that you and I could take a beautiful moment over there, before you claimed to me I want to invite you so we can pass it very well you know we should not to wait until the night when is the most beautiful, but is when the young couples go over there, because they deserve to have the most beautiful moments because that is done mainly thinking in the youngs.

Spouse of the president of the isle – My love, if you do not invite me now, would reproche you later, I am happy too much that you have think this moment with my person, is that for that I love you so much? I have love you, since that moment in what we stay without to say a word, looking to the eyes that afternoon in spring and that you told me, do you take a refreshment? Or do you want something stronger?

Rupert – Maria I have my car here, lets go to the lake, we also, because, no matter our man is not with us, we can make us the idea, and of to share it, is better even not to have him, because each one would be pulling by an arm.

Maria – I the truth do not remember the last time that I went to a place like that, or in another way, this is something that will make good, let's go before you go to change of opinion, get in, and come.

Roberto – You will see mister president, all will come after us to pass it well in this place, lets take this ship here because maybe there are not enough for all here, but you will see, I suggest that take this room for you, because since here you may go up and down to all the floors and to watch the views that each one offer besides nobody will bother here, this the most intimate en the all zone, because also since land you may find places to pass very romantic, my girlfriend and I for example no much come here, more we prefer to stay in that cabin at the border of the lake, where there is a risk and the water do not damage it, when it rain hard.

President of Venezuela – You Roberto know very well this island, you know even its more hidden places, because Worm never told me like that, he only told me about this cabin, and the other at the ocean side where the fishers stop to prepare theirs working equipments when return and when are going to fish.

Roberto – That is a magnificent place for to intimate with your couple beside have some corners where the fishers do not interrupt not even with speaking or with their presence, there is not better places where to separate from the world, and let you really alone. My girl friend is very romantic, you will know her when we go to Margarita, because Worm is going to get the permit and with the verb he has I trust that he will do it, no matter I have to married her he says, that is something that I want anyway, but maybe does not need to be so festinated, that is something that we like to do slowly.

Presidente de Venezuela – What do you eat you guess, Roberto? Here are all, they came one after the other just behind us, it will be because of us or for the beauty of the place? Because the truth, I desired to stay alone with my loved one, now it will be a share alone.

Spouse of the president of Venezuela – Do not sulfurated my love, that I what desired is to be here with you, and that I have it, that other couples or friends come here be here too should not to be motive for refuse but pick up yourselve, because what we want we have it already, always that we can share with them, if you promise to not make business conversations, give me no matter nevertheless two hours of your life, because you are mine, and can use your time the way I pleased.

Worm – Please, that nobody interrupt you on what you were, we do not want to interrupt, how good you pass it please ignore us as much as you can no matter it be for a short time, but share whatever you want because no matter you ignore us, we will stay here. Only that we know how to ignore you for example when I see Berta, there is nothing else what to admire, because where we should to point our angle of view? Is not to the most beautiful? Because that is my Berta, that is the most point of view she looks as the diablo himself that is who try to deceit us with its beauty all the time.

President of the isle – Mi heart, so long time that this place had build, and is this the first time that we come here, maybe is that I lost my romanticism, pardon me my dear for to ignore this paradise that I had for lost.

Wife of the president of the isle – It is allright my heart, finally we are here, and it is on what should import to us, you had too many things in your head, and I forgive you that, but the truth is that give me a lot of happiness that you withdrawl from work, for me I would desire you live it already.

President of the isle – It look like we think on the same way, because I was thinkin to live it for to go to Margarita, but the truth is that I will review his work at the return, and if he does fine, will live it with the character of permanent already, because I wish from my heart to be near you all the time, I was missing you very much, and worst of all is that I even had realize about that.

Roberto – This entire group is going to Margarita? If it is like that we have the advantage to enjoy over there, I feel shy for the others.

Minister of Venezuela – The president escaped from the isle, but I realized, but did not before that don Manuel to be ready to live before so that since Dona Perla was ready, we left to over here, They did not let us behind for a long time, and tell us that they were here, and came inmediatelly, the president of Colombia, is alreado in Margarita, they are says that enjoing and making room for us, he sais that he will separated the all flor at the hotel.

Don Manuel – What a beautiful place is this, how is that did not celebrated your weddings here? This is a place yet that Dona Ruperta's but no more beauty. This should be a drean for a wedding, isn't it Roberto?

Roberto – I really think like you, but rather to listen to my girlfriend before than you for that, because in it is her moment, more than mine. She will lose that day, which will not recover never ever. And will desired always to be the preheminent voice for the day which need to prepare for to deliver something that will bring a extraordinary satisfaccion and a enourme change in her life.

Berta – Roberto and me are agreed in many things but what he finish to say is very sense, and I unite to his opinion, as the poison ivy to the wall, that day is totally female day, at least the persons decent and prudents, need yield all our rights to the woman, that at the final of things is that will change her life, the man only will have a change in attitude, but basically that.

Miss Ruperta – What a man so condescendient and comprehensive came out to be at the end my Roberto, I congratulated you for your words my dear nephew, if your father would be here, would be saying the same as me because those same words, and he has we both, to Mary and me, both virgins for our weddings for our nights, and to both he found as a decent woman should be.

President of the isle – Here my substitute is missing is that I need to be able to say that I feel very happy, with him I will not think in to work, for what I have for living, Don Tomas, where are you? I am looking you everywhere and do not reach you and either and now I am listening you.

Don Tomas – Mister President, I am sat in your chair right now, thinking how do I will fill when you go on vacations. This is great, to be the president of a country, if not even to pass by a filter of a political party, or need to even pass by a people that could give its aprobal or refusal, only because the other person have decided and appoint me that is great. Could not imagine that could be so easy like that.

President of the isle – Ah, you feel yourself important, that is a little worry, that position is for one that feel small, if you feel great, maybe the position fit too great for you, be careful with your alerts, don Tomas, yes, that is the most important position in the all island, and come to happen that is received suddenly and in advance, yet you will have to pass for the filter of the selector Commitee for the president, that is pending, is not to be a definitive charge until pass by it, that is vital, please, think well so you may act well, I will go on vacation tomorrow, you are not definitive in that position, there are another three candidates, and need you to be more simple to be choosen as a president, never is choosen an arrogant person.

Berta – Mister president, I suspect that you will have the leader voice in the trip no matter this be a vacation trip, tell me If it is light that, we will go in the morning, in the afternoon or what have you think in your plans?

President of the isle – Dona Berta my daughter, how do you speak to me, if you know that I never act on that way, I will be the last in to take decisions for that, all of you should be who take the ones going ahead, I will only follow you, because my Talita and I desire to rest, and now you want to put myself to make calculations and all that? I thing not, the young always have much agility por things like that, in this way I think that if you need one with authority and young, the president of Venezuela should be the quarter back in this game of football, and no myself, that is the man.

Worm – President of Venezuela, what do you think about that is building on your back against you around here, is that you haven't realize of that?

President of Venezuela – Do not interrupt, that my lady and I are passing here too good, so once again, do not interrupt because to live some vacation for another, to whom is that interesting? Of course, not to me, we were to leave the past Monday and we did it, we went first to Colombia, where we pass two days seeing how much they have advanced in the installation of the system, they have advance so much, that they went ahead of us, they have already 10 cities entire working with the successfully system, and still abroading it, my vacations are still here, where my lady is very pleased, and have no hurry for to change this, but for only to get to know the kiosk at the border of the sea, and even not need hurry either.

Roberto – But that is a lot better during the night, I recommend to live for over there about the six o clock or later, not before, because you will need darkness to enjoy of the place.

Spouse of the president of Venezuela – Thanks Roberto you are always very focus with your advises, very appropriate knowledge and as he is so taking in love around here, I know that he is right.

Marina – Where is my Roberto? Hear, do not hide, that is you who I am looking for, do not pretend to be a foolish, because I know that you are not and I know that very well, where are you? Now, answer me of give our relationship for finish, did you listen to me?

President of the isle – What happen to you, relax, Roberto speak too much of the preety you are and how taken he is, get calm, please, because this is not an argue to win or to lose, this is a friends meeting and enjoy how beautiful that is this place.

Roberto – Is that Marina, you do not want to get married to me or is that you are not ready? If you tell me no, I will die of so much shy, I am and will always be for you. How do you think I can hide from you from who I want to have at my side always?

Marina – Is that I love you too much little love, I get jealous when you go without me, and do you not understand me? I get really jealous, because I think that maybe you have found to someone that you like better than me, I think I am loosing you, I feel like that, no matter it do not be liked that.

President of Venezuela — If there is a guilty one miss, that is me, also is my lady, and I swear that your Roberto is very ugly as a woman, frankly I rather mybe my wife, no matter should be to see her, but I feel like that, that he is too ugly, uglier than what I see my wife, old, not because she have many years, but because are many years that I am watching her the same, so does not need to be jealous, he can not escape, after all, what he has not confese here to this group, that desire to take you to our vacations for next week.

Marina — How is that you are planning to take my Roberto on vacation next week, and he not even have say something to me up to this time?

Worm — Marina, con with me, please, comes, I am guilty, I will explain to you.

Marina — Ah, but it is you mister Worm? The one that is running around the world to install a system . . . democratic, is how it is called?

Worm – I have been talk to Roberto since India, Marina, he counted to me how difficult is your father, and for sure he will not see with good eyes that you go with your boy friend for a week together with married men, and I told him that I will handle that with your parents and with you, and that you will come with us no matter we have to pay a high price, as to married you before to leave, that is the reason that he has said nothing to your parents or to yourself, is to me who you need to claim. But be careful with to hit me, because the men reaction is to kiss the woman that hit him in compensation, so that you may hit me, but after that and against you, of Roberto and mine, I will have to kiss you in the mouth to be dispensed from the hit.

Marina – Don Worm, I do not think to punish anybody, but to kiss you and say thanks of thanking you, that you can not imagine even how much I have suffer all those days, I have notice my Roberto so changed, that I thought that he has another or that I had done something for he to behave that way so diferent, it was a great change and on top of that with that smile that made my mother to coment to my father in my presence, what is planning him, that look so suspicious?

Roberto – You see what I was thinking was to have you with me a all week, looking you in bath suit, in night elegant clothes, light clothes, and have you in the bed, to sleep with you, that will be unforgetable, all that was passing fast by my mind, and only with a girlfriend, now converted in wife, and so young, because tell me, what is your age Marina some fifteen of you already have sixteen?

Marina – For you I have nineteen, because a married woman is an adult legally, but actually I have sixteen hade it last week, but I am ready for you, in any ground and any place. I love you.

Miss Rupert – Mi nephew maybe do not deserve to a girl like you Marina, but Is not with me that you would married, but him, my nephew need a woman a little more relaxed, you are a very launched woman, you act as a easy woman, my son need a woman less volatile.

Maria – I love too much to my sister, I love you Ruperta, but I know her since she was born, and Roberto had communicated to me how taken he felt by her and how much he is attracted to her, and her for him as well, and not you or anybody else will separate those two. They are mine that is the woman of my son dreams. The only one, he never have spoken to me about any other, not for to be friends, she has only be his love and his dreams, about the legss or the back side of any other, only Marina's and is from her that he is in love with, and he has tell me so many times about that night in which he be with her as his woman, how good those dreams make him to feel.

Marina – Roberto you are the only man in whom I have put my eyes, and I am also the only female in which you have put your eyes?

Roberto – Well, no are you the only one I have look at, but among all that I have put my eyes, you are to whom fill all my expectatives, all others I compare with you, and you are the winner for all of them, I rather you, because you are the winner of my likes and my feelings, I have take a lot of sympathy since always.

Worm – I would like you do something for me Marina, would you like to call your father, to tell that you want to go with your boyfriend for a week vacations together with all of us, and that you are going to be cared, only that will not to disturb you if you want to have sex with my brother, could you do that for me? If they tell you no, then I want to get married with him tomorrow are you prepare for that?

Marina's father – Hello papi, yes, I am sat what kind of question is that you want to ask me mu...cha...chi...ta?

Marina – What would you like, to loose your daughter because a man wants to take her for ever or would you lend her for a week only?

Don Tomas — Again, what kind of question is that? Of course that is better to let you go for a week than forever, remember we love you very much, and why would come someone to take you for life? What kind of stupid conversation is that one? What kind of conversation you bring me over the phone?

Marina — Do not get offended dadi, is that your daughter is a little big and need that you take some confidence to her, only that, if you do not have confidence in me, you have it to Worm, that I know you love him and respect too much, is it right?

Don Tomas — Yes, it is like that, I respect him very much for the kind of person he is, and I have all the confidence in the world for him, and the one I can have for another.

Marina — Are you going to tell me that you prefer him, or do you want to tell to himself?, I am going to pass the phone to him, because you lasted too long to answer.

Worm — Don Tomas, you know my mother, my uncle, and more than that you also know my brother Roberto, also you know my wife, besides, what she is traming is that Roberto is going to pass some vacation in Margarita island, and your daughter Marina, will accompany us, and I was appointed to ask you in what conditions she will accompany us, if as the girl friend of Roberto or as his wife, because she will go anyway, he will respect to her if she goes as his girlfriend, but if she goes as his wife, will not put care if she make you a grand father, but maybe not, but will intent it anyway, you decide.

Don Tomas – What form to speak is that mister Worm? Of course that weddings I do not approved yet, not even I have talk to my wife about that, she is a child yet, she is too young to die.

Worm – That means that she will go as a girl friend of Roberto, and when she return she will be a virgin still, is that what you want to say? Because like that is how it will happen, other wise they will pass a better season, but is your choice we live it to you.

Don Tomas – Then my election is that she will not go to that trip, not in those terms, she is a minor of age she is a minor and has to ataint to her fathers decition that is all.

Worm – You have to married boys; get prepared all, because you are not leting Roberto goes without you, right?

Marina – No, I want you to stay here, and let your family go alone, that is what I want, because I do not want to get a sufferance to my parents, only for some vacations.

Worm – Let me your cell phone Marina, please, because I need to make a phone call yes? Don Tomas then, I will pay all the arrangements for that wedding, do I have to sign for you? Or you will sign free and voluntarily for my brother?

Don Tomas – Is that you do not have any ritht over my daughter, none

Worm – I am going to pass you with the president sir, with your permission, I pass him to you.

President of the isle – Don Miguel, you are deneing to your daughter, and to the brother of our hero the possibilities of to be happy, as soon as they can, don't you realize on that? Is that you have the all island on one side, look well, she will go to that trip with your permission or without it, what do you rather? To give her the permission from your free will or do you want to have your permission by the force of the love? What do you want? Give her your permission with your will, or without it? Because a woman always wins to a man …. Always, if you fight you wil lose, and if you are opose, either you win, think it very well, with calm, wake up, let her go for a week, or for life, Roberto will do either one, the diference if she will get back intact or not, if she take her for a week she will return with all her honor, because we will be watching, and will not let them stay alone at any time, other wise, the president is ready to preside the ceremony here or in Margarita, that will depend on your attitude, or also we can take you to the trip and your wife, then you will be in charge to take good care for her, she could live in your bedroom or in another at your choice, and you do not need to expend not even a penny.

Don Tomas – Mister President finally I listen some sense words, that sound well to my ears, yes, that could be the solution, that we go, or that my wife, and they can sleep in the same bed. That can be a solution, and is the one I like more.

Worm – Then, we take her borrowed for a week, and from the permanence you may speak slowly with Roberto, after we return, because to the truth is that she is too young, will not be at all a bad idea to let them grow a little, nevertheless not too much.

Don Tomas - We love Marina too much, and we desire that she always have the best, when she may have it. It is her immaturity for a marriage that put me to think, I do not refuse Roberto, only that they are too inmature yet, I think that they need at least a year more, they know each other since always, I know that, but one think is to be friend, and another think is to be in a love relationship, she is too young to launch herslf to the empty. Nevertheless they will be happy, they desired too much.

Ruperta – They can come to live to my house, if they want to get married, for me is not a problem at all, and they know they count with me forever.

Roberto – I know aunt, same think my mother, if that you support us in all, but here what we look is that Marina come with us to spend the vacations, and we got it already, I do not are interested in the terms, just I want her close to me together, that do not separate us from that season that will mark the diference for us.

Don Tomas – Dear daughter, do you have any additional plans? You are not looking the way to deceived us to escape and make married work while alone right?

Marina – How do you think so papa, I could get married to him and go, and do every think, or could do that here any time, we go freely to every where and I let him to touch me, so that is all, because I am a woman and he is a man, and we want to feel each other, but to have sperm inside, I want to wait, I love and respect you and respect myself as well, to have he inside I need him to married me first for in case that I get pregnant and he may be dead when our child get born, so to avoid penalities, I rather to wait. I do not feel I am mature for to love my husband yet I think I need some more time to get that idea mature yet, that is what I think, is that everybody around here want that he come to those vacations, and I am not in accordance that he go without me to those vacations, that is all I want to be with the man I love, only that, dadi I love you very much and I know that you with mister Worm would find a solution for that situation, the best one, or the worse, that is indifferent for me at this time, because this is a love relationship for everywhere. As the same as I was expecting it to came out I am completely happy, and now I will be even more happy than all I could anticipated, because not only will have to my Roberto, also will have to my mom and you, I will be with all those I love, this will be wonderful, we will go tomorrow early.

Don Tomas – Did you listen that, we will live early so it will be good you to pack something for a week, take some suits, that the presidents from here, Venezuela and Colombia, this will be some vacation for the high class.

Ernesto – The passengers that are living in this plane, come approaching, because maybe is going to be the first one living, because is the first to be ready to go, come already have a seat and get ready to take off as soon as possible, that vacation are at the point to start, and will be the first assuming them, come over we will be living soon, we will winn this aereal rally, the first that ever have celebrated around the world, come soon, and prepare not only to compete, but also to win to those slow ones, come, let's win.

President of Venezuela – What things are you talking Ernesto, do not you know that you should take to my friends safely? In your plane is going a girl named Marina? You respond me with your life for her. Is the girl friend of the brother of Worm, will be better you pilot carefully or who pay the consequences, will be you, are you understanding me fine, I am not kidding, I am talking serious, you are putting too much in risk don't you think?

Ernesto – uai mister president, you speak as you do not know me, of course I am a carefully man, and a man of respect as much as my work as the lives of our passengers, and that girl should be that little love that just enter now, beauty as nobody, delicated as an old flower.

Chapter 4

Roberto – you are calling old flower to my Marina? Pilot, I thought you were talking with respect, that is a little girl, too young, how that old flower?

Ernesto – Don Roberto when a flower is new is in mayor strength, when is old, gets a little disarmed and loosing its leaves, and easily loose those petals and that is what I talk about, not in the particular your girl friend, that God shut my mouth to say undue words, or with disrespect, under no circumstances I would pronounce those words.

Don Tomas – Do you see why I did not wanted that you come alone, where you expect the less, a big mouth show up and do not show up a real man to defend you dear daughter, taped flower, is that not all men now how to behave in front of someone unkcommonly beauty like yourself, is for that reason for which I am jealous and and keep you into your circle always so you get your respect.

Marina – Papa, I have been in the company of Ernesto several times and he has behaved correctly, if you make analyses his explanations he must to call to a delicated old flower. He is right, there is nothing bad with his expressions, please, not be so bad thinking, let pass that, maybe were the most delicated words but him does not falt the respect to me, he is behaving to his height levels.

Roberto – Don Ernesto, for a next case, could you think before to speak, so we do not have a moment like this again, please, use just regular words, that do not bring that kind of confusion again, will you please?

Ernesto – Yes sir. It looks like this is not my best day, apologize, please.

Roberto – I know you are a person of confidence and maybe you are a little tired, why do not you call your wife and we pass to pick her up in Caracas, so she can go to Margarita with us again?

Manuela – Thanks Roberto, thank you very much, but I will go to over there, I am here taking care of my husband, and there is nothing that he needs to you to continue reproaching, he is a correct man, and nothing have said to that little angel, as the girl Marina who is the youngest of the group, and besides is a beauty as a girl.

Roberto – I knew you were in the plane; it was only for him behaved more accordingly.

Ernesto – If you continue with that, from now I will behave as a regular private pilot should and do not as I been representing, because who is not correct to its level are yourselve, and so you from now show respect for me or do not treat me with confidence.

Worm – I was not here when this started, but stop let things with no importance to go, and treat only the concernment thems, whatever be, stop talking about that ya, because it is clear this is passing to damage a friend, with not need, Ernesto is a member of our family, and as that should be treated, that is the situation, and will be punished who ever do not understand or accept that and could to respect, I have speak already, better discipline ahead. Then, are there in particular for us to be hear waiting for what is not going to come, or really are there any other, answer me Ernesto please.

Ernesto – No Worm, none in particular, surely I are waiting that the president come out first and they are waiting for me to come out first, I am going to call to find out, because the truth is that we are ready to depart. Captain, please, tell me something, what do we wait to take off?

Captain of the other plane – I am waiting that you go ahead, that is the only reason, please, go ahead, and fuimonos then.

Ernesto – Very well captain, do not move from over there, you are living me space where this plane can go, that is why I did not moved to the roadway, please wait until you may see my tale please, before to move a little bit.

Captain of the other plane – Very well Ernesto it will be like that, I will go inmediatelly behind you.

Ernesto – Adjust the seat belts, straight your seats so you do not get a dizzy spell, because we are going already, they were waiting for us to go ahead, that was the all delay, but communication resolve all those little details.

Act follows the planes get in the roadway to take off, and inmediatelly take speed, lift the nose and take off at maximun speed the pilot that have the presidents of Venezuela and the isle just got his license, and in reality what were waiting was that Ernesto a pilot with a lot more experience with more than ten twosend miles of fly for his youngest from which flu transporting to Worm to everywhere, once saw how he did follow and did like wise, because there are persons that learn the things on the right way, wait for another to show the way for they to do like wise, for which if the one in the front comete a mistake, also will comete the second.

Worm – The look we have in you my dear Ernesto, is that you are normally awake and resolve any inconvenience that to be present, because imagine waiting for nothing, only because is waiting that you guess that he is waiting that you take the iniciative, that sound very foolish and until a little humilliant, are the reason because Ernesto you receive more agreeable notices, because you act as an intelligent man, and that is something very appreciated for the people that have reach certain levels of success in life.

Ernesto – As you are a little curios, or maybe can speak to the president so he informe you what is the hotel to what we should go in the island, could you call by radio and ask?

Captain – Please, we need to know to which hotel address ourselves at arrival in Margarita, do you know or do you do not know, otherwise, please ask to the president of Venezuela for if he does not know, can call to the president of Colombia who is in charge to resolve about the hotel.

President of Venezuela – We are going to stay in the same hotel Sheraton, same hotel where Berta and Worm stayed to start whith their honey moon that I imagine they will having until the childs come, because as you know, really is when the honey moon finish with the guagua, that those bring behind the arms, and inside the mouth every time we want to concile some dream.

Captain of the other plane – Said the president that in the Sheraton, that maybe this trip should be to finish their honey moon, that I imagine that is happening, over there was started, and should finish realized?

Ernesto – Yes my captain, entirely, very gratefull for the information, over there we have the group completely informed then, where would be the president and the minister of exterior relations and their respective wifes, with that we complete the group on vacations.

President of the isle – Never travel in private jet, this is my first time.

President of Venezuela - On this case, is the same as a commercial one, because is coming full of persons, but the big diference is if you come alone or with one or two people only, now is like a commercial one, this plane is designed for ten people, and are coming ten people, is full to the capacity.

Minister of Venezuela – The first private plane I flu was when Worm that time we went to Colombia and Panama and then return to Venezuela, the second was with Don Manuel and here I am taken again, don Manuel is like my father, been that the original was taken by God he let me him for I do not miss him, not mine, because I feel very loved, so loved as I felt with my own.

Worm – That is Minister, it is like that. He love you as your own father, the same way your father use to love you, I did no see or ear it, but I notice your relations, because he treat you he told me the same as his elder son, the one in charge of the vineyard that are the family business. If there is someone that still need affections, to cry now to be saciated, other wise to stay shut until is needed the caress and lack of affections, because have still and if not, we should export to Africa, because over there there are love and affections, that I could not get in any other place where I ever have gone ever before.

Ernesto – How fast pass the time, when so well accompany, we can see the shores for our destination.

Worm – Once is enough Ernesto, we only needed the first time; we do not need to repeat it, none to look for a substitute, softly please.

Ernesto – Have no worry, I know the water is softer than asphalt, but today, is going to be upside down, remember that we flu long hours to every where with no problems at all, ya, please live that moment already buread already where it is now, give it for dead, please.

Worm – Good grief, Ernesto, it is seems that you do not tolerate a jog, not even from you nearest friend, you know you did not did in purpose, because you are a good pilot what happen is that experience produce a tetric afraid, and do not tell for the afraid to repeat it, only that, it was only an ugly way to remember an event that at the end of account nothing happen, not to the plane not to the persons only to the bandits that intent to assalt us.

Ernesto – Be quiet that I doubt much that have reason to be afraid of, the mechanics that to give maintenance to those planes are persons very serious in their work and very trusty, because they take very serious their work.

Berta – My life, we are arriving already to the airport, we overflu the beach where that accident happened that already past, did we live it behind?

Ernesto – Seat belts please, very tide, especially those that still remember the accident at land that we arrive to the roadway for landing, ya, we are going to land in a second we softly touch petroleum and road over it very briefly.

Marina – Don Worm, have faith, you are a man charged with faith, that the Almighty God free you from all bad things that the soberaing, that the man in general have designated launch, but you have the protector acud more powerful that the world has and have put you to our isle for to take care of that malefic and giver to do damaged.

Roberto – My dear love how do you come to talk like that you were a close admirer of my brother, you have touch the neuralgic center for his moral structure, you have sing a truth that he could not be able to undu under any circumstance you have hit the center of the Diana my dear heart, you are beauty and at the same time doted with a lexicam very florid, and a mixer of words very delicately fine.

Father of Marina – My Marina is a little girl full of faith Roberto, love her very much, not what you say, but love her with your heart, let me tell her that is a very little girl with a very great value several times her weight in comparison with what may value that weight in diamants finally sanded, that Is her before men, and in front from who know how to valuate that, and that would be at final of account who will be the one who judge to every one, to her and for sure will have her in a place of much preheminence.

Mother of Marina – I think much as my husband, she came to the world virtuose full with those spiritual values that now posees, I particularly do not feel any kind of afraid in to respald mi little dear daughter in any moment, because I have faith and believe in her because until today's day she has not give any signal of detour of on what she has choosen as her north in her habits of the use of the word.

Worm – Very well dear brother, Roberto, I believe that you are taking a great luck with Marina, who adore you, she loves you with all her strength of her hearth, she is tide to you as the ivy, how the oister close her capsule to protect the treasure that she save in the center, a genuine perl, valued as herself, protect it, with a tremendous power, so you should protect her your Marinita dear, because she is valued so much as the oister to the shell, so should be your shell to protect for her, with a strong force, that only the love may produce.

Ernesto – The president of Colombia called me, that they wait for you with some serape bottles, and some bottles of chilen wine to celebrate our arrival, he told me that hurry up, that the mozos have in the trays of service, and may fall down do not want to let rest, because are several bottles and are very heavy , do now want to let it rest, because they have orders of the president of the chain of the hotel to be ready for when you arrive, stay holding them that way so we should arrive soon to allow them to rest.

Worm – If you have hear that stupid think, do not let the tires to touch land, what are you waiting that we do to put an end to put remedy to so much stupidities, because that stupid order, be from someone that do not show any apretiation. It is acting with an abuse of the human being summit as are the waitters.

Schuaaaap!!!! sound the tires of the plain at to touch land, to start to calm the waiters of the hotel charged in the terrace of the hotel's bar that await for them to celebrate a courtesy brindis as a welcome that have our friends with a great hurry for to consider them to be persons of good will and that the waitress does not need to be under that pressure for the hotel, because it is not necessary, did not should be submitted under such pressure, they are not fisiculturists, a loaded tray should be sostained with both arms and let to rest over a table or counter until the time to comsume the time to start the brindis, then Worm says that will complain in written to the office of the hotel in New York so be dispatch instructions at the end to attack that stupid order that at the end arrive to ourselves.

President of the hotel chain — Be welcome mister Worm, and all your friends, and family, and persons of renoun that make the honor to visit us in those days, starting with this day, what agreeable notice received last night in my residence in the hotel of New York, where I live and where was lodged until to received such an agreeable notice, be all of you very welcome to this your house, where I am sure you will pass your more happy days in your entire life, that is what I hope, and is what our equipe of service will work for, so you may enjoy your days with us, yourselve and your distinguish friends, filled us with proud and satisfaction, dign of the most altruist labor in the world, that only God himself could dedicated to do that, because it was him who created man and did not make them to suffer, but to make them for to live with the best possibilities of to be happy, and that happiness to be past to others and to anothers, and so on.

Worm — Mister president of the Sheraton chain, I want to thank you very much In my name and from my friends and partner of travel, partners about the constitution of the system economical Democratico, in each of the countries honoring on that way to the memory of my father, creator of self for the order of me by God himself who comissionate him a long time ago, and left the labor half finished, hoping that his son, be who to continue it in his name, and in the name of the Creator of the universe, as certainly the owner of the hotel had mentioned, thanks for the hospitality and really yes, we are ready to pass a good season as well as you anticipadly said and have promise do your effort so we have that satisfaction, so, please, have some tolerance with us because at to say the truth, we have joy with anything, and probably make some unnecesary noise, so, you will not make a great effort with us to have joy, we are happy people already.

President of Venezuela – Mister President of the Sheraton chain, several months ago, came mister Worm to spend his honey moon with his wife, Miss Berta, and I made personally a reservation for they to spend those special days in your hotel, but they show up and at to arrive here, there was not reservation for him, that thing let me in bad situation with them, because that reservation was really confirmed and they denied it to him, so my name was not honored by your working team. Today I want to present a complaint with your business, I was waiting to find in front of myself to a person of the high direction of the hotel to make this declaration comlaint, hoping it does not happen never again.

President of the chain – Sorry very much that you have that experience, that was a personal decition personal mine, I just wanted to honored to mister Worm, giving to him my more direct hospitality, so I had did it today, the same way that he has given his hand to our country and to ourselves, rebuilding In a single day two of our hotels in the city of New Orleans, putting them back in service in less than 24 hours after the great damage that our hotels suffered, with loses more than on hundred millions, and we did not lost a single guess all were stayed with safety in our places thanks to his initiative at the proper time, what would last more than six months, in normal situation. Once again, THANKS DEAR WORM! also it is necessary to apologize with him for the possible damages that the troops of the United States could make against to his country, and to his personal properties, target of our troops, and nevertheless, instead intent to damaged us, he protect us, and keep doing it with his economical system that do not affected us yet, but have help our broke government to keep America in a freedon place, once again, THANKS DEAR WORM! We want to say the same one thirt time for his initiative with the people of the continent of Africa where also our business have property working every day better, and the great welfare that the people from that forgeted place in the world are having right now, and the welfare that they will have after the implementation of the Democratic economical system, because I realize they will do, right?

Worm — Thanks for bring that to mine attention, at this point, not yet, we are waiting a little for their economy be more stable, because as you know, their income per head, was very poor, the worse still around the world, right now they have a lot better welfare, because they are starting to produce all that they need to have a good life, we expect their economy be stabilizise in a few months and is when they are going to start with the system, just before they start to improve with their houses, and all that.

WORM!! WORM! ! WORM! ! GO!

Worm — This is a representation of the people, is very beautiful, but I do not deserve any recognition, the money used was not mine, actually, I did not have or had any money at all, the money was and is from the God Almighty of the world, the ideas used were not mine either, but from the same person, and the only one should be render honors, and that been is not me, is the God and father of the all world who is the one who deserve the all honors that are not few, and with those who want to be my ego to grow, I am not deserver of any honor, not even of a milk sugar candy, if the waitress want to do me the honor to serve me that desert, will really appreciated very much, because no matter I do not desereved to have it, I want it very much, so please me? But maybe I do not deserve those things, are so good to have it, that I want to ask my God to forgive me because I do want it, please forgiveme for that, please. The God father put the formula to make the serape and I order the construction of the all necessary thinks to manufacture it, and here we are,offering it to the all world, but not competing with the pharmaceutical companies around the world, they continue manufacturing their poisoning thinks, and the people who never honored the God Almighty are still using them, and our sickness that come from God himself are due to our bad attitude that I invite to every one to make a review to act in a better way, to follow God, instead to the Deavil, who is responsible for the manufacturing of the poisonous think that cure some, and start to another sickness, making you to fill bad anyway, and at the end remember we all must to render account to the Allmighty God, so I ask you to improve your ways, and act in a better way, pleasing yourselve, your neighbor, and to the God himself.

Ernesto – Do they will have chillos enough for all of us? Because I would like to be include in the list of those fish eater for today, and the best option that I see available is that fish for the meat and for so delicious that it gets, do not imagine how it would be that it take the season because is a fish with so much meat like that one, that it does not save a relation.

Berta – It is been so long that does not eat it that the truth have forgotten I will also will enlisted to eat it.

Marina – After what Roberto made me to work last night, I will see myself to eat one also, so have the amiability to put me for one so destroy it.

Roberto - I also should to reinforce my energies that my very dearest Marina have me to lose last night, that was fenomenal, we were busy was the all night my love?

Marina — It is not for su much, not even was penetration, only a game.

Roberto — A question, what is that you wanted, to me entired, or only a little part?

Marina — No my life, the breakfast, that is what I want to have inside. Breakfast I do not want fish, but would eat some arepas, or something like that, what about some cachapas?

Don Tomas, Marina's father — What is that you comment so much over there? It will be that you are needing that you to get married before to come here, according what Worm the day before yesterday, because I am listening some commentaries, the truth is some painful for me to hear, look like my Marina is taking borrow with Roberto, please be honest with me, tell me the truth.

Marina — No papa, only we past a long time kissing and embracing, only that, you can probe that I am still a virgin as when I was born, sex is something that we will have after married only, never before, that I promise you.

Worm – Sirs, please have some consideration with the others, stop talking over those themes, that are build only for the intimate alone, plese, stop talking about that. It is lunch time, and that should not spoken during this time, because could cause an indigestion, be careful because an indigestion, be careful, that an indigestion is something ugly.

Don Manuel – We brough some bottles of wine, my hearth, where did I put them, I do not see them for anywhere.

Perla – You do not see them because they are still in the cases, in the plane they should be, we put them in the cargo area and over there should they continue, I will call the pilot to confirm.

President of Colombia – Mister Worm, it will be that you and I and the minister of the exterior to have a moment of conversation about the program, or are you too saturated of that to occupy your mint again with that?

Worm — This are vacations, but I am a young man, I want to say that I am still, but at the speed I am going, Berta is going to put me old very early, because she is keeping me busy too long time, what thing get you worried mister president, tell me here and now, because they will can not listen you I also speak restrained, and know that I also speak soft, they will not listen.

President of Colombia — A group of narcos that are treating with to destroy and ruin us as well that will not stop under no circumstances, that always they were more powerful than the government, that do not make any effort for to combat them, because first will fall us in front of them.

Worm — Maybe will be necessary my presence before them mister president, I know how to confront them, and how to win with no violence at all, from a form that maybe you can not even imagine, can we make an apart to go to Colombia and talk to them?

Minister of Colombia – I think I can invite them to come over here, maybe is not necessary to dedicate a all day what we need is if they bring an army as they treat to could cause an great deal of damage here, and we have the hotel almost full at capacity and the neightbors hotels as well, gave us a little of work to get a all floor, we could get that some guess to be moved to another floor and some to move to another hotel to be able to get the space, all is very busy.

Worm – If you have any form to communicate to them, make them to come over here, because for sure will not like to spend the night over here, surely would like to excuse the very same day, for sure would like to return to their country the same day, no matter be night time, call them you come over here, if you want treat them, menace them, tell them to come ready to play the life here that here we will be awaiting for them with the venezuelian army and the army of the island, and to play it as they have menacing you that they are stronger, tell them to come to measure forces for once and forever, that we will be awaiting that come ready to kill or be killed.

Minister – Mister Lavandier, please? Good morning over there, this is the minister of foreign relations from Colombia, how are you going over there?

Mister Lavander – How are you going minister, are you calling me to surrender, are you going to leave me alone, or you still need to have some demonstration on our side?

Minister of Colombia – How good you put yourself the theme of the violence so early in this conversation, because it is exactly the theme, here in front of me is the paladin that say to be stronger enough that no army can stop him, I have it in front of me one that can defeat that the United States navy with whom have not possibilities to talk yet, but who is positively stronger than you.

Mister Lavander – You are on vacation in Margarita and you want that we go to overthere to kill too many innocents, on different forms, we are killing them, does not make any diference, if they die for an excess of consum of drog, or for an intoxication of plomo, what is that you want?

Worm – Give me the phone minister; let me talk with him for a minute. Mister lavender, what I ask of you is if you are strong enough to beat me of if you are one lose tongue who does not know what are you talking about, if you are a powerful man, show me your power, and come to get me, you have men with good experience as snipers but I am sure it was with toys only, come and get to a real man, can you get me or not, I think you are a chiken and nothing better than that, I defied you to come with your all men and see if you still can survive, because I will put to everyone in jail, bring all men you are ready to lose, or bring to every one and you will have a big party in the jail, I will live you until tomorrow at noon, if you do not show up, I will think you are a hen and nothing else, you are a coward but your presence can demonstrate that maybe you are not, but if you still do not come I will think that you are like those things deposited in the latrine. Come to finish with the bad life that I am having, I am having such a bad life that more is better to think that I am dying while alive come and finish with me, before the president of Venezuela that is killing me come and finish with the governants of your country and part of the government around your country big man but cowards, you are nothing else than a hen and one of the most cowards,you do not put eggs, because they will such a bad quality, that every one eating them should be afraid to contagious your coward attitude.

President of Colombia – Worm, is not being that you are extralimiting? You spoke as he to be a child this is a bad man, perversed, he is not afraid for nothing this will pass over you, do not stop to asesin as many as he can is a perverse asssassin and will make a very great damage, after the form you spoke to him, forgiveme for my intrusion with you.

Worm – Mister President, look like that you have a very bad memory, do not you know that as molest he be is as easy is going to be for me to defeit him? Have you forgot that I defeat the United States, France, Itali, Canada, Japan, Germany and some other more combine and at the same time, that they invade us by sea, air and land at the same time, and I myself alone, and will come that big mouth to scare me? We will not allow him to do that and do not worry that I myself can with him I alone will confront to as many as come with the power that Jehovah of the army will proveil.

Minister of Colombia – I feel a little coward Worm for to involve you in our matters, I feel terrible bad, please, pardon us.

Worm – I love you, and do not feel bad for to solicit a friend to be at your side in moments of need, do not be afraid they will make no damage to persons or property, they are not be able not to scratch me, or anyone else, do you remember when the king Ezekiah was invaded by Senacherib, what happen the next day, one hundred and eithty thousand of their enemies were laid in front to the walls of the city, all death, he wont the war and his soldiers not even move. That is the way God figth against the bad that disturb the people that are under his protection. And you are.

President of Venezuela – Mister Worm, I have an equipment to ear conversations on a large distance and could listen your conversation with the Colombian Guerrilla for to come and arm the war over here, in the vacational center of my country, and how do you think that I am going to offer myself for they to come and arm a war here, in the vacational center most important of my country, how do you think you can abuse of the confidence I put in you. Please, call them back that guy and make your war some place else, please.

Warm – Mister President, you are my friend, my family, and as you are I love you, but exist beside the old proverb that said to a big bad, big remedies, and no matter we need to assassin it will be a convenient bad. But I am sorry I do not work that way, but under a more pacific one, you will be able to watch by yourself how to win to a bandid, a bad bandit, we will win with a very sweet if we want to say.

FINISH WITH ALL AND WITH EVERYONE!!, Destroy all, kill to every body, do not let any one on foot, kill them all.

Minister of Colombia – Worm, that is the voice of lavander, what is what we will do now, he came ready for to destroy it all, please do something to fix it.

Worm – What do you think that he could do? I do not risk to him to take my blood out, not absolutely nothing, and I do not even move from here, waitress, please, bring me two beers please small and two sour lemons cut in half, please.

Waitress – Right away mister Worm.

Lavander – Let's go Carlitos, put a bomb in the parking lot of the big one's, explote those big and tall buildings, those with more occupants.

Carlitos – Lavandier put the bombs and only escape smoke, a little more and cannot even to escape myself from the parking lot, but nothing happen, all is fine, but the explosives did not work, only work as artificial fires.

Lavandier – Tomas, go with your group and murder to all those persons you can find in any building of hotel, finished all, and take any think with any value and destroy every think, finished up, at much as you can.

Tomas – Chief, the arms are charged with coconut candy and chocolate, do not fire, we found several pictures, we shout coconut candy and chococlate but does not get to them, only a few inches of the canon mouth, we pass a knife by the neck to the people and ony hurt to my partners, we are as in a rare world.

Lavander – A big group goes and destroys all you can find on your way, go, and show them.

Juan – Come sir, you come with us for the good or force, take with the chair, complete, with the use of bullets if necessary, shut Pedrito, do not worry, kill that dog, killed so, he does not dare come to defy us again, not him or nobody else.

Pedrito – Mister Lavander, try to kill Worm and only hit my partners, nothing was that I could do, the canon of my rifle AR-15 fold and now is pointing to me directly to the chest after finish with all my partners, this is as something diabolic what is happening here, I do not understand nothing, I am living here.

President of Colombia – I can not believe what I am seen, you, sat on that chair, while the delinquent finish with all, will not give peace in the all day to any body over here, he is finishing, there is a group that Is coming to kidnap me, do something or I will let that them kidnapped yourself.

Worm – Nothing will happen to you, calm yourself, not to me either they cannot make any damage in the island, the only think they will do is to burn petroleum that their plane expend, only that, there is nothing they could do, why do not you calm down and have a seat to talk, have a drink with me. Lavander you are under arrest, given yourself as prisoners, President and his minister, you both will come with me, and will make peaces, we will aply the electric chair in the field, bring the all true.

Worm – He is coming with it from Bogota, why do not you surrender once for all, haven't you discover that it is you that is just a little les than nothing". Surrender and deliver those arms, that you need those secutity guards from the hotel because you are scared always in the dark nights? Deliver those rifles already do not make me to repeat again because for each time I have to repeat it you will lose a finger of the feets or the hands, you only have five opportunities, before to follow the example of the kunta kinte, but be as you want.

Juan – Mister Lavander, help me, I am missing two fingers of my feets, and also my hands, cannot walk fine like that, will have to surrender, cannot, I am falling if try to walk, I cannot, I am falling.

Worm — Very well, I am putting myself on food mister, let's see what is that you pretend to do with that poor man, what you do not have done anything that is done necessary to stand up. Now call to those paralitics to take charge of yourself, mister president of Colombia, how much would you pay for they to deliver this garbage tided so you can make then to pay for all what they have make done?

President of Colombia — Two millions of dollars, mister Worm, until that I will pay.

Worm — Sirs, come and get two million dollars that are offered to capture this subject, it is surrendered already, only have to deliver him.

Worm — Mister President, I think that you have a debt to pay with those two gentlemen that have a package for you, or think to leave it here?

President of Colombia — The government of the United States is desiring to have those in jails so they purge a condem under their care, and I do not have any objection for that because could not desired that they return to their play in Colombia.

Worm — I told you that the narcotrafic will finish with the system, that together are not compatible, because the violence and the peace do not go together, necessarily have to go separated.

President of Colombia — Now only have one narcotraficant in the country, so our population could enjoy the peace, and in the foreign also can enjoy it, what I know is that the friend will be ready to collaborate with us to finish with this that is something that I need to find out. What do you say friend Worm, because you are a lot more powerful that all my army together, all my soldiers you can more than theirs.

Worm — No, not myself I am a man that can to be consider weak, I can not lift not even a sac of hundred pounds very well, with a lot of effort could lift it to the high of the chest, but more than that, very . . . very laborious, weak, barely could finish with a good man but one alone of the bad could destroy me quickly.

President — But that sir brought more than five hundred men, and you finish with them, only you.

Worm — No, sir, look very well, on what you see, say and do, I did not anything, who did it was the Lord God or the army, who did it easy was him, from the heaven, the Almighty, that yes is potent, that yes can much, I can say that he can it all. That one yes, he can do much, I could say, he can do It all. In that one is where I put my faith and my hope that is my power and my refuge. Is who never get tired, do not hit the bullets or nothing else.

With that enourmes exhibition of power and desenvolment, all the presents stayed atonits, surprised, for the quantities of things that the friend Worm could do without his friends could have acces on not even to something like that the exhibition of power and strength, how had dominion over those beens that consider themselves powerful and owners of the country, but owners or the evil that insommetable over them that we feeling the owners of the world, the boss, and who were in control for over all and alls, but at to confront with the truth, that truth that make then more powerful than them, were wining the force of the good for over of the power of evil.

Marina – You surprise me, Worm how can you do those thinks, to dominion over those beings, that have dominion all, and alls for the power of the force of pression of the evil, and whithout any kind of movements, without hit then of nothing, you dominated them just because yes, without on the way, without to have not even inmutated, and they stay completely dominated, you surprise me, how can you make those thinks, and we can not do something not even close to those things that you make in a natural way.

Roberto – Mi marinita, my love, there are many thinks that we can not understand, for example look, what size were us when we started to grow, to start to be a child, the size needed to seen in a microscope, and converted little by little in sometimes 6 1/2 feets sometimes, other less, but that diference so great since a particle that need to seen in a microscope, to convert in something that measure more than 5 feet of size. Is not this a proof of we are nothing? That one being can more than you and me? It woud be that we are close to nothing? That for more things we try to do, there is another that does more great things than us?

Don Manuel – Really that is the truth Roberto is ritht, on that; I think that I get in what I do not know, but is this a proof of that we are nothing? That one being can be more than you? Is that we are near nothing? That for many things we do, there is another that does other things greater than us? Really that is the truth Roberto you have all the right on that, I think I got involved in things that I do not know, but yet the unknown get with a strong dosis of information, so we know that we do not know, nevertheless that information we have, now we capture the information that we do not know anything, at least we know that, from there the wise Socrates extract: "I only know that I do not know anything". There is in the world quantities of information that in comparison with the known dates, those things give so much, that gave nothing, from there is that we do not know anything, how much know a new born, how much an ancient, our capacity of reception is great, our retention of information is like that great.

Miss Perla – Have not you realize Manuel how is that Worm could dominated to those beings, he did not hold any arms, or the legs, is not afraid infringed for anything, is an afraid that send on the distance, is a dominion at remote control, is not this really exceptional, for example the Mesiah, what was him, a son of God? Was him God himself? How may we be able to see, with the purpose of undertand it?

Worm – Do not say the sacred scriptures, and sacred because speak about God, that the

Mesiah was a prophet of God and what do that means? A prophet of God is a person who speak the word of God, is say, God say something to him and he say to us, is like a tape recorder, stored the information and repeat it, that is what a prophet act to do. We do not listen what God say, we do not understand that language, that is why the Bible say God spoke in my heart, and I listen...cannot ear with our ears, because we do not understand that language. God is spirit and his words do not make a sound that we can ear. The abstract does not make an audible think, to our ears may comprehend, the silence that spirits say, we cannot understand, when a noise is made in the air, the air make some waves that make the sound that is translated to our ears but in the empty a noise does not get translated, so we does not ear it.

Berta – Why if you are mine, I can not do anything near on what you do? What explanation do we have for that? Not are you my husband, how they say my maridin, I cannot do like you do, what difficult think are so difficult that we can not comprehend. What a weird sensation that we cannot cacht it, they make incomprensibles things to our understading, and nonetheless we have them very near to us, you may have it, but not me, cannot touch me, like if you have a superior capacity, or maybe only different, or different come fron dos=di=2? (All means the number two)

Minister - We could make those theories for weeks, for years. And maybe can not extract any information, that could bring to a conclusion that we may have a compressive conclusion due to our limited understanding that our doted of understanding is also limited, until our capacity of dominion and reason.

President of the isle – There are groups for example among those that are less civilized, that speak and who stronger speak is who have the word, really I appeal that keep the word, who can a more satisfactory answer, who can speak not the most delicated, but the most sens, represent to give us for to clear the theme that more satisfaction could give to a more satisfactory one, the one who can put in clear the theme with the best satisfaction, those who have to claim the right to expression, express themselves with the low voices, and due to tha lack of power gets the right to speak, due to the others in orden to listen, shout their mouth, liftting you to speak, as I do now, talking as the level of 3 decibels under the environmental noise, and all others shut so the most docil can listen.

President of Venezuela – The world is complicated, for that is the significative is the intolerance, and the pardon, to me look like that they are the nobles values, for over all other together, to trample is wining suddenly, and who finish triunfant is who forgive, who admit the strong and the weak, the world is changing and adaptable, and we finish understanding that all is relative at the cristal you use to see it, at the moment and the circumstances, all is relative at the moment of it.

Spouse of the president of Venezuela – The relative then is also relative to another thing, and that relativity will not bring to the creator of the relativity, all the relative do not have to be with Einstein, may have to be with something else more concrete sometimes, but also is very idealist, as that of the languages, that depend of a sound, we want to represent an apply or a pear, or a guava, that are practically the same, but that they taste different.

Don Manuel – This of the conjectures and the igualities or differences I think to ask, what have you think to do at this respect, in the east, Asia and the South? Which are your ideas and plans now?

Worm – Really don Manuel, because you give the impression of have stay in Africa, but sometimes in the world talking about so much relativity, do not help just helping, also sometimes there is the need and is created more prejudice helping and living like that, sometimes the people have need of been help, sometimes the people have a plantation filled with bad herbs, but do not take them out, pay attention, lend him a machete, or the chemicals for to another can do it, do not performed yourselve, because all depend of the kind of help that another require, for that sometimes it is necessary to meditated.

Don Manuel – That is why is spoken about Napoleon, which uses to take the time always he has to take an important desition. Because not always we should to move faster, sometimes is faster something that initiate slowly, or that the main decisions, need to be weighted more firmly doing it with calm, and finished more and better, the teory of the relativity come to take its place of a new account.

Minister – Listen so many things that depend, sometimes we give pass of what we have to expose your ideas, but life do not express not only that can be and energy expended, sometimes consume more energy to retain something than to express it.

Chapter 5

Worm – Considering that we should not launch against the other, only because we have considered that they require our help, we have decided to let them to pass until we have concluded that is something that they need and to desire to be supplied for them. In this part we have been try to the all the strong countries in Asia the economically solid countries and for what they do not expect much help in terms of money or its substitutes, because this serve as much as to buy or to pay the seeds, and to pay to who plants them, we could conclude with that you could deliver the seeds so they plant the grapes, and how good, did they told you that they want to plant grapes or your grapes? Over there is where radic the afraid, that is the solucion, or the details wich you need to confront? Make sure first, avoid insults this could be pacific or could be tormentous, not would be well sure on what is the most prudent? Not always work that to put in someone else shoes, because it could be its feets to be soft or callous, how are the other feets? Soft or callous?

Don Manuel – What is that is in your mind? When you came to the islands in the south of India? Those are really which will need more help?

Worm — See you the Africa for instance, I launch myself to send killed animals, and alived, the killed ones they are going to eat them with no protest, you send alives to grow up, multiply and then eat them, but what about if they eat them? What do they will have to eat later? Is this what is in your mind? But, what is in theirs? You are looking that they wait but are they in conditions to wait? Do they will wait? Will they make it? It is not on what do you want, also have importance what they want and what do the can, Minister where had you left the famous wine that one on which you motivated me by the way, or is don Manuel who have it under his control?

Don Manuel — No, that have not get down yet, that stayed still there in the plane cargo area.

Worm — And it should be that should there still? Should be that one the corresponding place? Wound you like to enjoy the delicious taste of wine that don Manuel manufacture?

Ernesto – I do not know, I think that you want I do for yourselves? Are you trying to weedle me with something for me?

Worm – Well, fine, I think that both things, that you bring us a little of it of that wine, and to join us to find out if it still is so delicious as usual, or if it has changed for the better or worse?

Ernesto – Well with respect to me, I will look it, and whatever be if I taste of not taste.

Worm – You see Ernesto what is the reason of what the president of Venezuela hired you to be his employee and do not of the airline for you worked it? For your service spirit, that vocation that very few have, you lend yourself to be up to date for that all that is required as necessary, you assume quickly and even without thinking or meditated, you are up to date and alert always.

Don Manuel – But in all those poor countries of the south of India, in those small countries or big, do not need to much agriculture or catle whith which we could help, what for really do not finish been the most poor or needed of the all world.

Worm – It will always one that would be the most poor country than all in the world, besides always would be one that be the riches, pretend you that I get involved in the lives of those beings, that could have a bad character, even worse than the Africans, many times I have been tented inclusive to go back from the Africans, have not been an easy job, that have result maybe have been for that they have so much attentions for with us, because no matter of have been helped in their marked north in our help plan have been out cociticens who have marked the bad note, are those from the country that we sent with the animals and the seeds who have paid the note, the always have been complaining, remember Erick, how he speak of the treat that he receive from they always how he was practically in all the sunshines, how was him always desiring the down at sunshine? How he was missing to return to the island, and have those soft days, that to have to confront to those nights in Africa.

Don Manuel – I am still thinking that if we could help to those poor persons of Asia besides, would be a very desireed labor, remember that the Africans offered to help to those poor countries, that they will offer the seeds, and also the new experts in agriculture and catle as well, and also that they all what were at their grasp for another will not pass for the all terrible situations that they had for a long time, that they were so long time, that they will be ready always, and I also are mister Worm.

Minister – You also have me, friend Worm, I also are ready and available, if you see in the case for ad me into that campaign that don Manuel have in the center of his two eyes, I also could get with cobras, and with any other malign thing that show up over there, my experience by Africa and the things that Erick has count me of what Africa was when he recently he arrive, to take charge of the production over there, how they eat, how saw that the African how they pass hungry, they use to make a food for two days, and little by little, were advancing, when they finally to make one daily food, they launch songs of thanks to the giver, then they bettered even more, they make two meals daily, bad food, if that can be call food the peals of the fruits, they ate the peals of the oranges, the peals of the plantains heated with water, Those are things that seen them you do not desire to known them.

President of the isle — When do you pretend to get back to the regular work again my dear son? Also I may unite to accompany, because since now only the poor countries you are missing, the richs in your way according I have see the map are very few and many of them are not interested not even to give an opportunity of to be convinced, do not desire no kind of act of conversation in that sense, they are denied by complete, they do not want not even a conversation.

Marina — Worm, I see that you are alredy very busy with Berta, she solve all your things, and needs, but beyond is your work to deal with those difficult asian, and you may need a preety face, a soft face, and beautiful body as mine to help convince to someone else.

Worm — Have you ear all what we have talk of those persons here and that all I have tolk before, that I presumed, that they would be very difficult to convince because their uses have being to form with blood and with fire, but besides with hurt, bloody and painful. You want to come to the danger, now in its majority, you have form beliving that they lien for a numerous group, they are persons that have been formed with fire, they are as a sword samurai, that do not know to be afraid the surrounding do not means nothing for them, is the same for them to fight with one or ten because is how work the karate, only that you do not stay in the same place, move and will only fight with one at the time, be agil or be agil.

Worm – You habe bring me over here to past it this season of vacations seen just start the part most algid of all the process of work, and feel now as if the now my desire do not advance, but by the contrary, that something invite me to stay, for this zone of easy work, because speak and talk as I do, not In this group that speak and act in a different way, that frankly, do not bring me desire of to stay behind, but the bad is that I have to render counts for those acts, thanks friends, that you do gests of be brave inviting me to reasume our labor, and now until the beauty sister in love is including herself in this tonality, that herself is including, I already have an owner, you are very beautiful, and it will very easy to fall in love with you, but what do I do with Berta? I should do not change her for nobody, is the one that God put in my way and is the one that fall in love with me, I am not going to change, not even now, and less now that think to make a family by the blood and for those and for the one who cry for to receive compassion.

Don Manuel – I am still thinking in which is the date in which we depart to Asia, to help in all those that you may need help so they do not pass hungry, or any calamity as those that Africa had during so many years, Worn what I am asking myself is if you will lose the afraid invade you and let you down in a chair forever, or if you will return to life let me tell you that you want to seat, that boy that is at your side and have and feel its streng, those you show us in the past months when overfly yet in the skies of Africa, we will go in your place, and that God protect us, better in your company, but that your company . Will not accompany, we will go without you. Know it.

Worm – what friends have I found, do not know you what is the moment to advance and what are the moment to stop? Do not remember the wise Solomon used to say many time that there is time for all in life and in dead, that the is time to advance and time to go back...

Don Manuel – You repeat properly, you have lived well, is now the time to advance, tell me please, the number of Erick please, mister Worm, that could be tour contac to know when to start this advance.

Worm – Caramba, you are really determined to go to Asia, you really are. Good morning my dear Erick how are you doing over there

Erick – Worm?!it is Worm! !it is Worm! Caramba, how things are going over there, how are those vacations, are you having a good time over there?

Worm – Erick is also agreeable to listen to you to talk but here I have to don Manuel and the minister, surely you do remember them, are determined to go to Asia, and the purpose that they have in that trip would I say a litle suicide, but will not be without your help and collaboration, of course, because I know the kind of man that you are, of your preparation, and dedication to the work, that when you start something do not separate from it, until it is finish.

Erick — You know that are not only words, look for example, when would you pick me up for to go over here so we go to Asia? Do you have your plans or are starting to prepare now, do I expect for you here tomorrow, or am I too fast?

Worm — We do not have date in that sense Erick, would you give me some days here, taking a little of rest, maybe they want go at little ahead, I will pass it to you so you put in clear that concept.

Don Manuel — Erick are you ready to continue with your labor in Malasia, I think that we can help very much over there, where there are a group of beings taking advantage of a mass extraordinarily poor, but I notice to the friend Worm a little sat be maybe better to live him to rest I know he will reunite with us is not going to abandon, I know that will not happen, good, we count on you, we will pick you up the day after tomorrow, we pretend to arrive tomorrow, and will spend the night over there, and will go with the sunshine next day, so we get to the destination near noon. Prepare seeds of plantains, orange, and others, all you can put together to plant over there, please Erick Worm will stay here resting a little and for sure that will joint us, he is not the man that sit down, he is a man of intense action.

Minister or the exterior of Venezuela – Hello Erick, speak the minister of Venezuela, I also will go with Don Manuel, we wil joint tomorrow in Central Africa, will stop to sleep, then will stop in the desert to depart to Malasya.

Erick – How good, we will have a team then all will go well, with the wind on popa, It is okay that Worm rest for some time and come some time later, any way he have never come at the beginning to the work, always some time after a lapse of time of intermediate, is when he always get present.

President of the United States of America — Good afternoon sir., this is the President of the Unites States of America, I understand that you are preparing a cometee that will go to Malasya, poor country in the Asia, with the purpose of to help them as you did previously in Africa, and I do not want to stay behind, I want to express that count on us and any other neighbor that you may need also, that the friend of them is always our friend, because will have too, will not to be alone never more, call me with anything that may be necessary, call that, men, machinery, seeds, equipment, anything we can collaborate with, call me to this number that you now have, this is my direct number, and here you can find anything that be necessary.

Worm – Erick, this is Worm again, I just finish with the President of the United States, and he offered me any kind of collaboration that may need over there, they stood at the side of the previous project, but that is where more resources there are available, and now do not desires be indifferent no more, that participate with any help that they can cooperate with, and they will answer same way as they have being , that at the time to count, count with them, please, communicate with me what you may need.

Don Manuel – Worm, we are prepared to depart, do you stay always, or have you think go soon to join us.

Worm – it is very well don Manuel, I will pass two or three days more over here, and after go to you, and then you the meeting in China to continue then to the south.

Don Manuel – The economy is not that bad as it was in the Africa, but nevertheless is a country most poor over the world at this time, with a little push that we give them will finish with their suffering.

Erick — Where do you suggest we start, or what don't should we to talk first to the responsible to direct the agricultural and cattle for in coordination with them direct our actions, getting that way all our activities be going and do not come to find obstacles in place of find contraries, find alliads?

Galio Gauchan — I am the comissionated of Africultural and cattle, welcome to Malasia Sirs. I understand that are aliads of mister Worm, the one that is developing to Africa, and are coming to help us in the development of our country for consider that we are one of the countries more poor and give of the world, and in your opinion we need help desperately.

Don Manuel – The true we do not know with how much desperation may you need help, but yes, you may be needing that someone give you some support, in those moments, we have a very powerful allied, when just last night sound the cell phone of Worm and was the president of united States, offering his help for the countries that remain in the world and may be in need of help in order to install the system democratic because of their poverty. They installed already and have the all America with the system working, we only need to add Africa and Asia, and we are going south for the world to be all integrated and functioning.

Galio Gauchan – Very well don Manuel. What we need is that you offer to us the necessary seeds of the different cultives that you may have, so that we could plant them, completing on that way the, production that we may need, as plantains, casaba, potatoes, oranges, and a variety as that, I know that you are an expert in plantations of grape and the posterior process to make the different kind of wines, I have receive some reports since Africa in the North. Where they plant besides, melons, watermelons, and some similar, can you help us with that?

Don Manuel - yes, of course we can help you on that point, we have with us seeds for the different styles of wine here with us, we brought Erick, do we have them here, with us?

Erick – Yes, Don Manuel, we have tree or four different kinds, available at the instant, do you want I bring them?

Don Manuel – Yes, I think that he want them already to start that group he has over there, behind those brushes, mister Gauchan we have those seeds here and now, do you want them now, or you are not ready? All those trailers are for you, all that there are bananas, plantains, cassava, and some more, that we need to see in order to use them.

Erick – You look someone completely independent, why do not you take posesion of the seeds that we brought so your people have enough on what you may need, on that form no need to be with the pending for one side, and on the other side you can dispone on what you may need. When you may need them, look that we are not here to importunate you, but in order to serve you, is for which we invite you to feel free, we do not want to make any gest of imposition, but you to feel free by complete, whatever we can do to help you, we will be ready always, all the time that may be necessary.

Mister Gauchan – Thank you since I saw you around here, was desiring that you may mention those words, we are not given receive help from any person distant of our country, but of the locals are accepted in order to receive help, that make us to act with a king of despotic, is not only for you, is for any foreing person, is an automatic reaction that we consider completely normal for us, we always try to be independants, and really that we pass quantities of needs, but goes with idea of do not disturb, to others, because we accept your collaboration, later you will come to solicit ours, and maybe we are not ready to help you, for do not want to loose what we have for to give to a foreign.

Don Manuel – Does it look anormal what we do, but we do not come to look for anythink of what is yours, or what you have pass in order to get it. We do not come to look, we came to give you, but it is not either that we need to make greater efforts but either, we are bringing what we have, we need that you get our confidence, that you trust us, and on what we do, we do not have any interes on what we do, do not wait anything in return, or any pay on your side for what we now do, this is completely disinterested, we only do the desires that our Lord, he wants that you and yours live their lifes without any kind of carences, that from the all good things things that there are in the world for you and us to enjoy, we have it in abundance, so you do not be looking in a foreign home, on what you may have in your own home, and to not need to envy on what together may have, any thing, you also have it.

Mister Gauchan – Don Manuel, you offer lots of trust with your words, those are soft to our ears, sound you as our own family, and I feel really ready to accept you hand as a friend because I feel that really you really have come to help us from far to bring us your kindness and the good that we really need.

Erick – have you realized of the quantity of thinks that we did in Africa, those were that most poor countries in the all world all the time, never knew country that need so many things to be able to live correctly, with a good quality of life, the most indispensable they were in lack, they have the pain of do not to have anything to be able to feed their bodies, they could not make their clothes to hold the cold the insect were rounding their bodies for the lack of hygiene, are things really vital in the daily live, is for that, we solicit that to accept us, that to give us the opportunity of to be able to subminister things that are extremely necessary for your people. May we count with your help to be able to help you?

Gautan – It is alright I will trust you, will bring some collaboration that is at our reacht, but please, do not over pass from your line, and do not abuse from our gentile.

Don Manuel – The worst think we have in our behave is that we have too much sens of humor, we make too many jogs because with that we gain a lot of fun, and we may contagious until you, and to any one who is in relation with us, but only with the intention of gain a little of happiness, it is the only reason to look the good sense of humor, never we have the intention of to hurt or to make damage, we are persons completely morals, only want to help. We could to have the every think, we could to stay in our respective homes and over there to have it all that we need, we are here not for us, but for you only, and the only think we are expecting is that you allow us to do what we came to do, and to receive it with the intention that we offer it to you, we a good spirit of solidarity, allow yourselves, to know us, allow yourselves, let us that we can do something with no interest for you, the only think we need is the thinks to do well to the body, like to eat, drink, take a shower, wash our clothes, nothing extraordinary, just normal thinks.

Gaitan — I told you already that it is allright, do that you want to do, we give our support with the condition of that you never will moke of us is our only condition of poors, because we are poor and we apparent that we are, and do not want to change that because we have learn that the happiness is in the simple thinks.

Erick — The leader of those ideas to share our kindness with the world is our friend to whom have been called Worm, he is resting of so much dedication that had have in the last years, for example he was dedicated to help Africa from the all thinks that without that without never come before, he learn thath was in need of, and without notice he send some containers containing inside the things that could do good and help in those things that are totally basics for the survivals, also took his good will to the richess country of the world, not with the final of giving, or loan, not, to help them to confront to itself the collaboration of a friend, when it was necessary. We do not went to consult, but to open a bridge of collaboration, The United States have been pass the all life taking to the world all that they have left, now we have try to open something and we give to the world what they need, no matter what they have too much or the thinks that they are in lack looking for the carencies of the other person when it appear. That is what we want to do with you, what we can see and to resolve, we hope that you many communicate what you need the most and we could not see, that you have the trust of tell us those carencies that you have hidden, for a reason or for others, but to give us the opportunity of put them to our knowledge, and after together we do it together we fix it, we do not pretend to come here and do all the labors that correspond to you cocitizens, but only to help you in what help you on those things that you alone would not be in capacity to resolve by yourselves, but to allow our hands to be at your dispositions and available for when to be good, look you for instance the Africa, what they were in need of, and how they are now, all those seeds that we brought are from them, now are them who put them to our disposition for you.

Don Manuel – We want to be your friends, and the only way that we want to show you, it is the only face that we have and the only that we expect you to know, so you see that we need one to anothers, would you have drinking watter available that you can suminister, please?

Gaitan – Yes, of course, inmediatelly we will give it to you, we had dry your mouth with so much you had to talk you need us to suminister something to fix that.

President of Venezuela – Friend Worm, I am asking myself, when do you pretend to return to Asia to continue you work of unification universal with your democratic system, because is not seen if I can accompany you in that zone, I there to offer myself for that committed, think that you think in that zone as something really pasionated, I think that is a little more imponent to what you yourself could to dedicate.

Worm – You want to accompany me in that trip to Asia mister President? Don't tell me that you pretend to live your people for that sympatic adventure, would I say, would you ready to slide for those territories of the cobra openly as you say?

President of Venezuela — So you know, I do would go with you, I would like much to see how you direct those conversations, at the time, is possible that a president of a country recently converted at the system could serve to support in that campain of yours, do not you think?

Worm — At the truth is that you know from where the respald will answer to the questions that they will see in need to ask. Completelly, the answer is that the possibilities of that you may to serve in that purpose may be very wide, mister president, there are in the island at the present time a great quantity of persons, since Nepal, India, Corea, China, Vietnam, Japan, and some more, several people from each country and over there, they are over there with the intention about how the system work, the actual president is attending personally and adecuatelly, have call to the president several times to consult details, and have answered over the phone, besides of what have answered questions directly to the visitors, also Berta have answered questions, when have ask for me, have manifest that they have me incomunicated.

President of Colombia – Senor president of Venezuela, I dare to suggest that let to the expresident that go with the friend Worm, because he may be a better company until inclusive to yourself, at least that you desire go on vacation, because in that sens, remember that are you the president of Venezuela, and your country are needing you in those moments of transition, the new system does not have time enough from the implementation and many questions can come that maybe you have never saw to know the best way to confront, so will not know the right answer, with the president of the island will not happen the same because they have that system operating a long time, and he already have live the experience to answer all the questions.

Minister – To me liked to go and to accompany don manuel to Thailand, and all those proyects that should be handling over there, it should be something novelty, because is not like Africa, here should be something more compensative, Thailand is not a country so retarded as Africa, but yes, it have much vegetation that they will need to make disappear, there are rain forest over there is what they have a long time back, that they make agricultural fields and the forest are no longer, on the way needed, others convert with dense forests and an enourmes quantity of rain, that still continue to fall over the forrest grounds that are over there.

Worm – Yes, that is like that is as you say, but nevertheless the fields does not are totally clean as in, and Africa, but the ones that are completelly clear with hierb remover or chemicals that is the form as they do and result much more faster of to make that Is the reason for they to act as they do, and the rain that fall is a lot they need to be fast and permanent, when they use those hierbicides, its effect is longer lasting, other way the rain does not allow to remove the bad hierbs in the necessary quantity they will need. Don Manuel arrived over there, he look for Erick and both are already installed over there and all the seeds arrived also the same afternoon there was a ship prepared in east Africa, and in a few hours will have arrived.

President of Colombia – Don Worm I have much appreciation, really, but do not count on me to go over there for that forest to compete with the wilds, cobras, and similar that in Colombia we also have some, and we do not need to go to know those ones from over there, with the evil on what we already have we have enough, and we are comform with that we already have it is enough we do not need to compete with the foreigners, besides that are men of the field, not men of cities, the guerrilla kill them, for is that we have the soldiers, and from some time someone should give up, well that the soldiers finish them or something else.

Minister – To me would like to plan a visit to Africa again, but I plan to go alone, I know they are not going to receive me on a different manner as they received over there with you, because that time they did receive it was for you, to us they did not give us your treatment, only when you were present, if I show up alone is going to be something else. The attentions that I may hope to receive will not be even samples of that time, it will be anothers, and in another way, I have no doubt about that.

Berta – Mister Minister, that was for the first time, do not expect that reception ever more, that will not be repeated if we go again, it will be of a minor impact, and if we go by the third time, the maybe not even receive us, it will be for our account, that you may have for sure, the humanity is not so elocuent or lose either, that was an exception, look that the members of the government asistied to a reception with us, practically push it, does not have come if the president does not demand that get presents.

Minister of Colombia – I also see the life with those eyes, do not imagine myself or my president involved in a conflict over there, for those territories forested or involved with wild animals ruds, like the tiger of india, not even in the company of those locals that I suspect they have a better relationship with those, maybe because they run faster than me, that is only the imagination, because in the real life it may be completely different to all we can suspect and could realize, because those wild can be salvages from any angle or point of view that can take effect.

Ex president of the isle – Worm, what are your plans in that sense, I am on vacations, if you like or require that to accompany you, I will do, I go to over there and the easy or the difficult that life be, I do not leave you alone never.

President of Venezuela – You are not alone, Worm, do not put that hard face or sat face, that we are your friends and we are with you, for the thinking face that you carried I see you very thinking, and that one is not the Worm I knew, my friend is a happy man and ready, and now found you sad and something light with the switch off, like you to be withdrawl from that intempestive campaign in wicht that you were involved.

Worm – Really that if I feel something left behind now, I no longer have that strength of the previous time, now I am more paused, I found myself on vacations, and does not want to make than the previous time that we suspend the honey moon for a large and festinated trip of honey moon, it was not as well as it should be, and is when we get back to reasume, and will not going to suspend it again for any reason that someone may alegue, will finished this days of vacations and we get back to the attack, we still have two more days, I now that the expresident will go with us and will make several meetings with several countries each one, and will get involved on this and shall continue, if we analize slowly this, and shall continue, are not so many countries or meetings various that will need to effectuated, and still we shall subdivide.

Ex-president of the isle – Yes worm we will go since here, I will call tonight to my president substitute so he take charge of the isle inmediate, and stay in charge as a nominal president, from once and forever.

Worm – That is what I was in need of, I think that yes, that back up is too important at this moment, you know that there is a defy, is something that does not dominated or either made me to hide, or make me to be less.

Ex-president of the isle – Good evening mister president, how are you passing it over there, how is going that position? Imagine that you know all the details that move over there, and do not have any problem to resolve all the little details, because you have a working team that solve the all things, and I hope that you be on top, because on this vacations just discover that I should to abandon that position, and that what I need now is to continue with something a little more of my was, of a ex or of now is not, or he was, or some like that.

Chapter 6

Yes, honestly, there was some things which I did not feel comfortable, but here with I did not feel well familiar, but with the advise, they have put me on the way with their wise advises and with opportune apparition of them, we have resolve all the things that we have could present, on the best possible way, now I have under my control, we can with this load that apparent to be very heavy? Do we have to call the next?

Ex-president of the isle – But you have no idea what you are given to me, because Worm and I are calling you for you to take position with a permanent character since already, I am going the day after tomorrow to vist Nepal, to visit to who was the younguest president in the story of the world, a little country that China invaded, and put to the all inhabitants of that place and later put in deportation previously Nepal was to some thousand kilometers at north, and install themselves just north to India, on top of the Himalaya hills continuing over there with their sanctuary same as usual.

President of Colombia – What I like the most over all for that labor is that is going to start early, while before it may start, finished before, and then the efforts are better, because they will get the best use of it. Those are laborious persons and when they get dedicated to something, to an end, do not stop until they finish it which is the truth.

Ex-president of the isle – With the all productive apparatus and of commerce , the work of the direction of the country should be something overwelmed, but as is so much the different suppliers, the final amount could not to be so numerous, in the final amount will result no so grave, not should be overwhelmed. Is not so grave really, it was wrong from the beginning.

Arrive the expected day for the president, we are on a Saturday day, and they are prepared to live to its to their first interview of the second day of work for this new section of the world, that they expect to be the most difficult due to the forms and ways of behave form and diferents to ours of to do thinks, but to finally take a decision and depart for their destiny, Worm knows already what is waiting for him, but the ex-president does not know anything about how to handle thinks, it will be a surprise for him.

Worm – Will be called equal, or it will be called him ex-president?

Ex-president – You can call me Tomas, that will be a lot easier, and I will start to fill with an enourmes weithg changed of my body for the floor.

Worm – Good morning don Tomas, I see that finnaly you awaked, I let you to sleep all you wanted, did not awake you, for respect to your behave in the past, and I could see that you look very tired, we are over Asia. We decided to come starting in the Pacific Ocean, that is a more near route that coming acroos the Atlantic Ocean and then from the all

Europe, and finnaly Asia just in the center of it.

Don Tomas – Should be Sunday in the morning.

Worm - You are very well oriented, that is exactly what it is we have this day for the initial route, unpack the clothes, and finally unpack ourselves, tomorrow will be the first day of the meeting with China the country most at the East the rest are India, Nepal, Vietnam, north and south, the Koreas, north and south, and some more at the east. How is your mind for this day, because with the luck of the simultaneous traductors this that are invented modern and its new technology, is how if not exit from our living room.

Don Tomas – Ahhh, what a different sensation, we are still in the hotel, here in Nepal, I felt so much peace, which I felt never before, land a little of God, because is to realize that he live here, together to the Dalai Lama, who start his labor been still a small child from some 6 or 7 years of age.

Worm – The Dalai Lama's automovil will arrive any moment, we should not have to wait too much he has the habit of to arrive early. We should then to suspect that his chauffer would be used to arrived early, and there it is as in the pictures of sales life insurance, exactly on time, ten to ten, Good morning sirs. Of this very important meeting, hope you have a good night and a good morning of this Monday day.

Congregation - ! Good morning mister Worm!

Worm – Thank you sirs. How good you awake this day with energy, I want to introduce you before to start in matery a change, that for me was bad, but for you goes into your benefit, we have with us today to Don Tomas, some of you have talk to him and others have seen him as the old president of the isle, that just was substituted because don Tomas accomplish already with the time he promised to serve as president, and just freed, he was more to the west before to arrive to this continent passing a week of vacation resting after 27 years or hard work ininterrupted, been this his first vacations but now we have him, inclusive for hour rest in this meeting, he will helping us also, with any detail that you may need, we will serve both, but he is the great expert.

Don Tomas – Good morning, that I think the most important and interesting from all that is the president from the local Nepal, the noble Dalai Lama, a Sir in our environment for an enourmes quantity of years for now, and continue been interesting, because he is always the religious what bring us to over here, and is always an interesting person for us due to its motive that is always a conversation with the Lord and that is something that practically nobody wants, because whatever comes from him, everyone despite it, summarily, it is him who offer the most and at the same time who everyone dispise, and at the same time, but I appreciate everything that come from him, and always receive with good desire. Very well, then, let's start from the beginning.

Dalai Lama – Good morning Sirs., to this very important reunion in which we pretend to install a system that is more in accordance with our form of operate our way, the encounter with Mister Worm will leave us this system for us much more in accordance with our new eschems administrative, more efficiently, the distribution, the jobs assignation, and if come to the case of expend, and all others eschems to have a better redistribution of all goods and services in all vertients to have a place, we are please, mister Worm.

Worm – After that all in the isle could see the different forms on how it is aply, and all models that we could find available, this system help us in order to be able to manage the administrative system in the best possible way.

China – Please, excuse me, maybe we are not those that more fast may learn, but when we learn we do it well, you say that with this system we may probe, as we saw in the island, and the administration of this model, over there we put all the details that we should control, and all the articles, and then we have disseminated and controlled, we search and go putting and supervising in all aspects.

Korea – How good are you here, we put you in groups for among all that the verify that the system function, after among as we verify that the system work and after among all of we make this exercise, we can give the system for aproved, only something that we do not understand, we can ask by electronic mail o by phone for you can help us in the aspects that can be failed, and can keep going.

That day they start to work in the mathematical and financial check out, with that purpose they make two groups by separated, they evaluated the world in its entorn the new way that the world is going to turn, on the other hand in the island start to organize the next participants and make two groups, and two more on the way, next to follow this, in a form of chain that will not stop for any reason.

Right away the make this group: Japan, Thailand, Cambodia, Phillipines, Indonessia, and all the islands around, if they forget a country, they just include them and keep going, but in the review they make the corrections, Papua, New Guinea, island Fiji.

Once they graduated the last group of countries in order to integrated worldwide the Democratic System, it is evaluate the world in its new entorn, which is estimated that will be very different for the nature have approved to address itself, and to straight it's new route in the best sense, the pronostics of performace for the execution and behavior of the Bible, is approved in the part of the Lord, approved to give the world a new hope and a happy end and a new life with better quality and more happy for all it's participants, talk to them every day with a great satisfaction, at notice how have on a way very united and all with a great satisfaction and partnership, they make everyday a reception for the day, with tea of leaves or cinnamon, others drink other kind, and others to drink coffee with milk.

The entire world wanted to participate of this report, which no matter the personal interest of the great mayority that liderate and dominated before the world, had to claudicate and leaves that the good finally to take the direction of the order of things. Being this the model that finally takes the leadership of the flag of command.

The world decided agglomerated, because the model of Africa suggested that the best in order to have a better administration of the things of the world, so they decided to make agroupations of countries for the different regions of the world, and so it was subdivided the administration of the world:

In the Asia they made an agroupation including Siberia, China, and all other countries that constituted Asia, with some strategies among all very healthy, been Africa who take the leadership and the better example of organization and among the could obstacles or way in that could find, decided that the love to the other will take always the leadership, and it will take the leadership, and be taken as the measured to put remedy to the conflicts that could present.

Europa decided to integrate by completed, and them all together could have an ardient harmony that they decided all to make inclusive one only language for all, as well as Asia and this resulted so agreeable that they did it for the all world, with only thone language to communicated easily the entire world.

America also, the all continent got integrated under a single administration but indicating that soon they will try to integrated the all world as a single nation and that the entire world speaking a single lamguage, that word not return to speak in a different form of communicate easily and do not discriminate, and have a brothership world wide for the eomomy wealth asking the blessing of the Lord that approve this way for a better world for all, that from there will have a single language, making the world to go back to the genesis how could and should be, the way as himself form the world to be, and in honor to the person that dare to motivate all to the change to a better world, the all world will remember Worm as his worldwide leader and decided to appoint the world GUSBERTA in the honor to that couple that work timeless, restless, and never stoped until they got that worldwide in which convert itself the hole planet, and a life in more harmony.

As it could be comprehend, the world was divided for cause of men and its conflicts, so that was to be expected that its conflicts will not finish and that no matter the maximum good faith that no matter this was converted in the only law over the humanity, to resolve the matters that did not allowed the communal life, but for over all, have a moral compromise for all, and this was the love from one to the others and vice-versa, and the all differences that could aflore were dilucidaded in a party for the democracy, resolute for the common good.

In every continent was prepared a kind of saloon for parties that was denominated Salamanca in the honor to the island where all started for the common good, that was the beginning of the system political-economic DEMOCRATIC.

All were in accordance in that all should stay and be as more united as a family should be treated, with love and understanding, with all the tenderness possible of a new born baby and this be the example to follow among all beings of the galaxie celebrating on this way unitary and global the **day of the Lord** and this day would be celebrated in every house for groups of friends, as the daily dinner, that were reunited for the commonwealth of those 200 visitors that the island adopt as regular citizens, models for to stay living in it, and be a part, and they to prepare those family groups, to share daily the food at the end of every day in house the one of the group and make it rotative instead to make each in its own house.

Before those happenings, Jehova look at the world since the place where have reunited in order to pass the time, until he could prepare the dreaming world where to share with the world so desired from him and that in language of human persons could say that was a little thinking and with the moral down before the actitude of the world, to which have dedicated so much kindness, and never would dedicated the necessary attention and dedication for that all the best possible life, with his protection and support, living each day as he always decired it to be.

But as he had loss all hope in this world, had renounce to it, and have been separated for ever, because he was convinced that will never would be to comeback to it, for which looked among his memories how should form the new world, because it was hoping the final of this in order to restart.

But one day raised the head and observed to the world that of course still have free will of decision and decided whatever he wanted, and started to see the good relation that was having one with anothers, and admired and said inside or himself: "this is the family that I always have desired" and what a happiness he felt inside of himself, it was like a happiness so great that could not have it in silence and needed to look to the beings that always accompany him in his desire to form that special group, and reunited with them soon.

He called Enoc, Noe, Moses, David, Isaias, and Jeshua, and invited to take a look over the world and to have a celestial food among them, after to look in what the world after to have all ready for its destruction and have change to this model of life, after so many intents, finally had got what he so much had desired, and the others before named God happy with him, and came down to earth, and look the deposits of Don Manuel to choose the best wine that so much have deleited to our heros and make a toast for those legendaries persons whom were the roots for which was feed the tree that form this teoric world that God always wanted that God always look for, and he was so happy that made a toast for the new world, as God said that day: MY **DESIRED FAMILY HAS COME TO ME"**

FINAL BOOK Author: Jaime Vinas

www.ingramcontent.com/pod-product-compliance
Lightning Source LLC
Chambersburg PA
CBHW071422180526
45170CB00001B/188